GREEN WITCHCRAFT GRIMOIRE

GREEN WITCHCRAFT GRIMOIRE

A Practical Resource for Making Your Own Spells, Rituals, and Recipes

AMYTHYST RAINE

Illustrations by AMY BLACKWELL

ROCKRIDGE
PRESS

Interior and Cover Designer: Julie Gueraseva
Art Producer: Samantha Ulban
Editor: Jesse Aylen
Production Editor: Nora Milman

Illustrations © 2020 Amy Blackwell. © Lucia Loisa, p. 73 (Tourmaline, Pyrite). All other images used under license © Shutterstock, p. 73.

ISBN: Print 978-1-64739-142-3 | eBook 978-1-64739-143-0
R0

For Roberto, my soul mate
For Nancy, a kindred spirit

Contents

Greet Your New Grimoire

Welcome to the magical world of the green witch and to this grimoire, which will be your constant companion on this wondrous journey. The witch and her grimoire are seen as a traditionally magical duo, just as much as the witch and her familiar.

I'm not so sure whether I discovered green witchcraft or green witchcraft discovered me but *"there's magic in the green,"* as the old saying goes. For a lot of us, it starts with herbal teas used for specific medicinal purposes and expands to using the unique magical energy of plants, herbs, and natural materials to cast spells, creating positive change and opportunities within our world. You'll find yourself acquiring, growing, drying, and collecting a plethora of herbs for a wide variety of uses.

How do you begin? Where do you start? There are so many different types of plants and organics out there and so much to learn about each one of them. You will find that a grimoire loaded with the knowledge you need is an invaluable tool in the practice of green witchcraft.

Use this grimoire however it works best for you; you can flip through to catch random information the universe is directing you to find. You can mark your favorite section, choosing the correct organic element, ritual, or spell for your special—or most often needed—intentions.

And while you're gathering all this new information, growing in your knowledge and the practice of green witchcraft, you'll want to take notes. You'll find space to write notes and jot down your own thoughts and magical connections with the plants, practices, and energies you will be discovering. You will be able to keep a record of spells cast, herbs used, results, and recipes for future use.

For many of you, this may be your first adventure in the magical world of green witchcraft, and you will experience a new awareness of the energy that is harnessed in the Earth's bounty. Those of us who have been practicing for any length of time will never forget when realization dawned, and we knew with absolutely no doubt that there is a power within nature, energy for us to freely harness and use for the benefit of ourselves, our lives, and the lives of those we love.

Nature and Spirit work together to create magic, a magic that will pave the way for your unique journey into the wonderful world of witchcraft, and this book will be a part of that journey for you.

Cast Your Green Circle

Many spiritual paths incorporate "sacred space" into their practice, whether this is a building set aside for their rituals or services, or sacred ground blessed for this purpose.

Below you'll find directions for preparing your space, as well as circle castings, so that you, too, will be able to create your own sacred space in the way that works best for you for rituals, ceremonies, and solitary connections with divinity.

SIMPLE CIRCLE CASTING

The green witch creates her own sacred space for doing rituals and spells by casting a circle, calling the four elements, and setting boundaries of stones, or salt, or candles, or cord. The space inside a sacred circle is said to be "outside of time." It is a vital start before doing your magic.

TOOLS YOU WILL NEED:

⁂ A broom

⁂ Candles: 4 white tea candles or 4 white votive candles

⁂ Sea salt

⁂ Incense: sandalwood, Nag Champa, or an incense of your choice

⁂ Matches or lighter

1. Sweep the floor for the area you've chosen, preferably with a ritual broom, but a household broom will work as well.

2. Set the white tea candles at the four quarters, also known as the four directions, an equal distance from the center of your space.

3. Pour a fine line of sea salt around the perimeter of this space, connecting the candles and creating your circle.

4. Light the candles and the incense.

5. With the pointer finger of your power hand direct your energy, and from inside your circle, walk it clockwise three times, saying:

   "Once 'round this circle to clear this space. Twice 'round this circle to bless this place. Three times 'round to seal the ground."

Simple Circle Opening

When you've completed the ritual or spell crafting within your sacred space, it's proper etiquette and common sense to open the circle, meaning to properly dismantle this consecrated area. To skip this step would allow energies called forth within this circle to bounce around the universe in scattered and undirected ways.

1. When you've completed your ritual or spell crafting within your sacred space, stand and face the north gate.

2. Raise your power hand, athame, or wand in the air, to the north quarter, and in one fell swoop, in a counterclockwise motion, cut a circle through the air, saying:

   "Disperse all energies contained here to their rightful place.

   Fare thee well, time and space.

   This circle is now open, releasing love and grace."

   What other ways do you open your circle?

What other ways do you open your circle?

_____

_____

_____

_____

_____

_____

_____

ELEMENTAL CIRCLE CASTING

This simple circle casting engages with the elements, representing them through carefully chosen stones and delightfully scented incense smoke.

TOOLS YOU WILL NEED:

* ☆ A broom
* ☆ Candles: 4 votives (green, for earth; yellow, for air; red, for fire; blue, for water)
* ☆ Stones: 4 stones, one for each of the four elements (a green stone for earth, such as adventurine, jade, or moss agate; a yellow stone for air, such as yellow calcite, bumblebee jasper, or citrine; a red stone for fire, such as garnet, red jasper, or ruby; a blue stone for water, such as blue-lace agate, azurite, or turquoise)
* ☆ Incense: sandalwood
* ☆ Matches or lighter

1. Physically clean and sweep the area you're going to prepare for your circle.

2. Set the four votive candles at the four quarters (four directions), along with the elemental stones you've chosen for each candle.

3. Creating a circle with the stones, lay them around the perimeter, connecting the candles. The stones don't have to be physically touching each other; a space left between each stone is fine.

4. Enter the circle. Light the candles and incense.

5. With the pointer finger of your power hand, direct your energy around the boundary of the circle, beginning with the north gate at the green candle, continuing around the circle, until you wind up back at the green candle, saying:

"By the power of earth, air, fire, and water, magic will be cast within this space. By the power of Spirit, its energy will be clear. By the power of the witch, manifestation is near."

CASTING WITH A WAND OR ATHAME

You'll be directing some potent powerful energy in the process of casting a circle. Your wand, or athame, will direct and focus this energy for you.

TOOLS YOU WILL NEED:

- A broom
- Sage smudge stick
- Candles: 4 white votives
- Essential oil: sage, peppermint, or rosemary
- Herbs: petals, blossoms, or leaves from an herb of your choice (optional)
- Matches or lighter
- Athame or magic wand

1. Cleanse the area that you've chosen for your sacred space, both sweeping it and by smudging. Sweep east to west, saying as you sweep:

   "Sweep, sweep with this broom, all negativity from this room.

   Sweep, sweep from this space, all negativity from this place."

   You may feel a tingling sensation on the soles of your feet that rush up the calves of your legs. If you feel no physical sensation, know that your cleansing is still complete.

2. Anoint your votive candles with the essential oil, and place them at the four quarters, or four directions, of your circle.

3. If you have chosen an herb, sprinkle the petals, blossoms, or leaves around the perimeter of your circle, while connecting the candles.

4. Light the candles and incense.

5. From inside the circle, take your athame or wand in your power hand and direct the point at the candle at the north gate, the gate of earth. You will start at this spot, and continue around the perimeter until you come back to this quarter and this candle.

6. As you travel around this circle, sealing this space, say:

   "By the power of the witch's blade, by the power of the wand, this circle is cast.

   This space is consecrated and safe. Its boundary sealed hard and fast."

CASTING FOR LOVE AND ROMANCE

Spells of the heart are extra special and the space that you cast them in should be filled with the right energy for love and romance. This circle casting should set the stage for romantic fulfillment.

TOOLS YOU WILL NEED:

- ☆ A broom
- ☆ Sage smudge stick
- ☆ Candles: 4 white votives, 4 pink votives, and 4 red votives
- ☆ Stones: 4 pink rose quartz
- ☆ Essential oil: rose

- ☆ Herbs: dried rose or hibiscus blossoms or petals
- ☆ Incense: rose
- ☆ Matches or lighter
- ☆ Long-stemmed fresh rose: white, pink, or red

1. Cast this special circle for spell or ritual work involving love, romance, or friendship. Cleanse the area you've chosen, both mundanely and magically, by sweeping and smudging.

2. Anoint your candles and stones with the rose essential oil.

3. At each quarter, set one white candle, one pink candle, one red candle, and one piece of rose quartz.

4. Use the rose petals, or the hibiscus blossoms, to sprinkle around the perimeter of your circle, connecting the candles.

5. Light your candles and incense.

6. Take the rose in your power hand, blossom down, and use this to direct energy for this circle casting. Beginning at the north gate with the north candle, continue around the circle until you come back to this gate, saying:

   "By the power of earth, air, fire, and water, within this circle may love flow free.

   By the power of earth, air, fire, and water, may this circle be sealed. So mote it be."

Part One

A WORLD FULL OF MAGIC

From the depths of the quaint cottage at the edge of the woods to the streamlined city life of an apartment dweller, you will find the green witch flourishing around the world at large. The green witch may have the luxury of land for gardens and growth and magic or may grow herbs and flowers in beautiful pots on the balcony of an apartment. The power of green witchcraft and the ability to be successful and happy in this practice is there to be embraced by all.

No matter where you live, or what your circumstances may be, as a green witch you will find ways to deepen your connection with nature, the magic inherent within it, and the nature spirits that inhabit this realm.

CHAPTER 1
Nurture Your Nature: Spells for the Organic Realm

Natural magic is not something we need to seek; it's something that we must learn to recognize because it's always just a breath away. You'll discover magic in the green-growing things of the earth, and you will learn to harness magical energy in tune with the very turn of the earth's seasons, solstices, and equinoxes.

SEASONAL SPELLS

In this section, you'll learn to take advantage of the earth's cycles and reverently mark the equinoxes and solstices with unique ritual and celebration. You'll also learn to tap into this energy for personal growth and fulfillment.

WELCOME THE WINTER

The winter season brings with it a comforting darkness that can be used to incubate and nourish magical energy for the manifestation of our wishes and desires. It's an introverted energy, quite unlike any other time of the year. Think of it as a magical cloak that shields us from the world's busier energies, enabling us to focus more clearly. The winter season provides us quiet time to reflect, consider, and plan our goals, directing our lives in a positive way, and preparing us in turn for the livelier, more vibrant months of the year. This spell ensures an introspective and fruitful wintry season ahead.

TOOLS YOU WILL NEED:

* Candles: 3 red votives and 3 green votives
* Essential oil: rosemary and cedar
* Table, window ledge, or garden
* Stones: moss agate and red jasper
* Herbs: pine boughs, poinsettia, pine cones, or holly
* Matches or lighter
* Incense: frankincense or pine
* Cup of hot tea or cocoa (optional)
* Pen and paper
* Small cauldron or fireproof receptacle

1. Create your altar space with the votive candles. Anoint each candle with the rosemary and cedar oil, and if you like, carve into them an image that connects to your intention, astrological sign, personal magical energy, or the name of something you desire to manifest.

2. Arrange the candles on a table, a window ledge, or in a favorite garden spot, and put the stones of moss agate and red jasper among them. Decorate this altar with the flora and herbs, placing these plants and pine cones in an outer ring around the candles and stones.

3. Cast your circle and light each of the candles.

4. Light your incense, enjoy a cup of hot tea or cocoa (if desired), and think about what it is you want to return to you along with the spring season. What type of change do you want to manifest in your life, whether with your career, a relationship, or something else unique to you? Where is growth going to be the most important for you from a personal standpoint or a magical one? Write it down on a sheet of paper. Take your time and relish this quiet moment of reflection.

5. When you're ready, touch the sheet of paper to the flame of one of the candles and drop it in your small cauldron or fireproof receptacle. As you watch the flames consume the paper and the smoke gently rise, know that your desire is fanning out into the universe and will come closer to manifestation with each new sunrise leading us closer to the next season.

6. When the ritual is done, extinguish your candles and incense, and open your circle (page XI).

SPRING YE FORWARD

With the dawning of the spring season comes the time to plant seeds of green things alongside seeds of hopes, desires, and wishes. With this growth-minded spell, let's plant and tend, and usher them into their fully manifested and glorious fruition.

TOOLS YOU WILL NEED:

* A flowerpot
* A bag of potting soil: should you live near a cemetery, add a pinch of cemetery dirt as well
* Paper and pen
* Seeds or small plants: in choosing seeds, consider what you want to grow and nurture:

    For love, plant a miniature rose

For keeping negative people at bay and positive people close, plant a white geranium

For prosperity, plant mint

For cleansing, plant sage or rosemary

For a heated, passionate love, plant chile peppers

For healing and good health, plant marjoram and fennel

For increasing your power of intuition, plant mugwort

1. What is it that you want to grow and nurture and develop? Figure out the answer to this question, and then purchase your plant or seeds.

2. Find a comfortable spot to prepare this spell. A regular outdoor garden spot would be perfect, but the dining room table will work just as well.

3. Line your flowerpots up before you and open your bag of potting soil. If you have it, now is the time to add a pinch of cemetery dirt to this soil, creating sacred ground in the process.

4. To enhance this spell, write down in detail exactly what it is you hope to achieve with this magical endeavor. You can write multiple goals down on one paper and have only one flowerpot, or you can create a separate flowerpot for each intention. Fold the paper into a small square and place it in the bottom of your flowerpot.

5. Add the soil and plant or seeds, water it well, and nourish it with care.

SIGNS OF THE SUMMER

June is a magical time bringing with it the energy of fairies and mythical creatures. Let's use this most magical ambiance to start a spell we can release over the course of the summer. Within this spell, we'll do some knot magic to bring us closer to our goals before this season ends. Be sure to time it during a still night with a full moon whenever possible.

TOOLS YOU WILL NEED:

⚝ Candles: 1 white pillar

⚝ Matches or lighter

⚝ Ribbon (9-foot piece) in a color of your choice

1. Consider what color you want to choose for your ribbon. This will depend upon your intention for this spell. Many use red because it symbolizes power and life, and use it if it suits you. If you are an adventuresome soul who's not afraid to express your magical preferences, choose a ribbon in a color that will emphasize and assist your intention.

2. Light the white pillar candle. With the ribbon, tie nine knots, every one holding the key to the energy required for your unique goal and the element of magic. **With your intention firmly set in your mind,** begin tying the first knot, reciting the chant as you go and continuing this empowering process for the next eight knots:

   "By knot of one, this spell's begun

   By knot of two, my words are true

   By knot of three, it comes to be

   By knot of four, power in store

   By knot of five, the spell's alive

   By knot of six, the spell is fixed

   By knot of seven, the answer is given

   By knot of eight, I meld with fate

   By knot of nine, the thing is mine!"

continued →

Keep this sacred ribbon in a safe place until you're ready to unleash its magic by untying each of the nine knots. The timing will be determined by your intention and how you choose to have this magic manifest. This can be done gradually, over a period of time, or in the course of one evening. As you untie each knot, visualize the successful manifestation of your magical intention.

FEAR NOT THE FALL

All during the spring and summer, for many of us our gardens were flourishing with herbs, blossoms, and flowers. Now, the Wheel of the Year has turned, and the time has come for gardens to rest. We're going to set the tone for the winter sleep, giving our gardens and ourselves a winter blessing.

TOOLS YOU WILL NEED:

- ☆ Candles: 1 white pillar
- ☆ Fireproof plate or cauldron
- ☆ Matches or lighter
- ☆ Incense: patchouli or sandalwood
- ☆ Herbs: dried herbs such as sage, valerian, or chamomile
- ☆ Mortar and pestle

1. Take your candles, incense, and herbs into a favorite spot in your garden or chosen green space. Be aware that the nature spirits who have fluttered about this space all summer, guarding it and keeping it flourishing, will now be growing weary. Bid them farewell, thank them for their presence, and let them know that their return will be anticipated with love and delight, saying:

   "I bid farewell to the spirits here,

   With the promise they will return next year."

2. Set your white candle in the center of your garden on a pretty fireproof plate, or in the center of your cauldron. Light the candle and the incense.

3. Add the herbs to your mortar. Slowly and gently grind and blend the sage, valerian, and chamomile. When you've finished, take this bowl and visit the four corners of the garden or green space, or the four directions, depositing a small handful at each spot. Silently bid the nature spirits adieu and wish them a peaceful slumber.

RITUALS FOR THE EQUINOXES

The equinoxes represent a perfect division of light and dark manifesting as equal hours of day and night. But as every green witch knows, the representation of the energy inherent within this natural phenomenon goes much further than that. The equinox grants us a chance to harness the power we need for personal growth within ourselves, and this energy is all about finding balance.

VERNAL EQUINOX RITUAL

The spring equinox has long been connected to fertility and growth. This bountiful moment is the perfect time to cast spells for abundance, spells to draw to you something that will expand your experiences, heighten your life, and fulfill you from the roots up. Call upon this potent ritual to do just that.

TOOLS YOU WILL NEED:

- An egg
- Small saucepot or pan
- Clear wax crayon
- Egg dye
- Candles (choose your intention and candle color accordingly):
  - White candles are good for all intentions
  - Green candles, for money and prosperity
- Pink candles, for romance and friendship
- Purple candles, for business success or judicial circumstances
- Yellow candles, for creative endeavors and communication
- Brown candles, for physical fertility and health
- Incense: Nag Champa
- Matches or lighter

1. Before the night of the spring equinox, set your intention. Boil an egg, keeping this intention in your mind while the egg boils, or chanting your intention over the bubbling pot until the egg is done. Let it cool. Hold this boiled egg in your hands and imbue it with your magical intention, reflectively considering what you want the final outcome to be.

continued →

2. Use the wax crayon to write on the egg, or draw corresponding sigils upon it, focusing upon what you feel is appropriate to your intentions and desire. Dye the egg with one of the colors above that corresponds to your candle color and your intention.

3. On the evening of the spring equinox, in a space of your choosing where you will be comfortable, light the candle and the incense. You're going to take this precious magically charged egg, and you're going to peel it and eat it. You can do this very ritualistically if you choose, before a spring altar and within a cast circle, or take this egg out beneath the evening sky and the stars and consume it there.

4. Know that as you consume the egg, you are embracing and harnessing the energy of the spring equinox and its magical propensity for growth and fertility.

AUTUMNAL EQUINOX WICKER RITUAL

The autumnal equinox embraces endings, peaceful conclusions, and periods of solitude for personal reflection and analysis. This day is also filled with the blessings and joy of harvest and gathering, of preparation, abundance, and a sense of security in the knowledge that the earth provides for our needs. Use this spell to mark the autumnal equinox and usher in rest, regeneration, and magical hibernation. Note that if space and safety are restricted, a small box, even the size of a ring box, will do. Your intentions and their strength are where your power resides, not within the largest basket possible.

TOOLS YOU WILL NEED:

*   Writing paper and pen
*   A wicker basket (such as one used for laundry, the size of which will depend upon how much safe space you have for a bonfire)
*   Firewood: enough to fill your basket
*   Lighter fluid or lamp oil
*   Matches or lighter

1. The day before the autumnal equinox, sit down in a cozy spot with pen and paper and write exactly what you'd like to put to rest in your life, whether disagreements or something that's causing discord, causing you to worry unnecessarily, is dominating too much of your time and thought processes, or is holding you back from success or goals, or anything that you feel needs to go to make your life run more smoothly. Take your time, time to reflect and ruminate, time to embrace the inner and honest dialogue with yourself that always accompanies this process.

2. On the evening of the autumn equinox, gather the tools for this ritual at a place that's safe for a bonfire, carrying your written intention of what you're putting to rest with you.

3. Set your basket in this safe spot and fill it with the firewood. Douse it with the flammable liquid and light a match to it. You can enjoy this quiet ritual, either by yourself, or with kindred spirits who are embracing the energy of this equinox with you. If that is the case, sit comfortably, share a libation of your choice, laugh, cry, reminisce, dream, and connect.

4. When you feel the moment is right, take the paper you've written from your pocket, and toss it into the flames. As the wood crackles and the flames begin to dwindle and die, know that what you wish to disengage from, what you wish to put to rest, will be snuffed with them.

5. So mote it be. The ritual is complete.

What other seasonal rituals do you like to observe?

_____

_____

_____

_____

_____

CELEBRATE THE SOLSTICES

The summer and winter solstices embrace our earth's divine opposites: the longest day of the year and the shortest day of the year. Whether sinking into the darkness or coming into the light, both directions embrace the magic of the green witch and life's infinite possibilities.

A SUMMER RITUAL: THE PRAYER TREE

The day of the summer solstice, besides being the midpoint of our year, heralds and embraces new beginnings. This could be why June is such a popular month for weddings. This solstice embodies the growing season, as well as the nature spirits that are connected to the garden, including fairies. Use these rituals to tap into, and connect with, that magical nudge toward fresh beginnings. What wishes, goals, or intentions do you desire to manifest with your prayer tree?

TOOLS YOU WILL NEED:

* Pen and paper
* Essential oil: peppermint or sage
* Yellow cord, ribbons, or embroidery thread
* A tree: one that grows on your property or a small potted tree that will make its home in a corner of your living room, or perhaps you'll plant a special tree for this very purpose

1. Beginning on the eve of the summer solstice, write your first prayer or wish on a piece of paper.

2. Anoint the paper with a touch of peppermint oil.

3. Using a yellow cord, ribbon, or embroidery thread, tie it to a limb of your tree.

You will continue with this practice for the remainder of the summer, adding your wishes, desires, needs, and thoughts to the tree. If this tree stands in your yard, the winds will come, and the element of air will carry these thoughts to Spirit, creating a special communication with the divine. The act of planting a new tree especially adds to the significance of "new beginnings."

A SUMMER RITUAL: A FAIRY VIGIL

When my son was a small boy, his midsummer's eve traditions included an all-night vigil under the apple tree in our backyard in the hope of seeing fairies. Beneath our apple tree, I'd fix a special candle for him, placing it in a cauldron along with some herbs to entice the fairies. One summer, he watched dancing blue lights across the top of our wooden fence until they dropped into the green grass of our lawn, where the next morning we discovered mushrooms had sprouted overnight, forming a ring, while the grass within this ring had withered and died. With this ritual, you can make a fairy vigil part of your own summer solstice tradition.

TOOLS YOU WILL NEED:

- Candle: 1 white pillar
- Essential oil: lavender, jasmine, or gardenia
- Matches or lighter
- Fireproof dish or cauldron
- Herbs: mugwort and calendula (if available, handfuls of marigold blossoms would be perfect)
- Chair or cushion
- Tea (optional)

1. Prepare your area early in the evening, before twilight.

2. Anoint the pillar candle with the essential oil and set it in your dish or cauldron.

3. Sprinkle around the candle, at its base, mugwort and calendula.

4. Light this candle and place it in a safe spot near you. Settle in for the night, or at least until the wee hours, when you can no longer stay awake. I promise that your experience will be enchanting, with or without a fairy sighting. You will find this night to be very revealing on many levels—spiritually, mentally, and personally.

A WINTER RITUAL: THE YULE LOG

The winter solstice celebrates the return of the sun on the eve of the shortest day, the one with more hours of darkness than any other. With the return of the sun comes renewed warmth, hope, growth, and life. To the green witch, this solstice approaches with the knowledge that, along with the sun, spring will return and with it the newly greening herbs and flowers that pave her magical path.

For those of us lucky enough to have a hearth, we can celebrate the return of the sun with one of the oldest traditions: the burning of the Yule log.

TOOLS YOU WILL NEED:

☆ A hearth or firepit

☆ Broom

☆ Essential oil: rosemary

☆ A log

☆ Herbs: pine, holly, bay leaves, mistletoe, or other seasonal plants

☆ Matches or lighter

1. To begin, clear your hearth, sweeping it clean of any accumulated ash.

2. Sprinkle the area with a few drops of rosemary essential oil and empower it with your good intentions.

3. Imbue the Yule log with your intentions for a healthy, happy future and thank nature for the bounty of the harvest you have reaped.

4. You can decorate the log with pine, holly, bay leaves, mistletoe, or some other plant that you connect with this season and that is significant to you.

5. As twilight falls on the night of winter solstice, gather family and friends around the hearth and light the log.

6. Welcome back the sun in deep gratitude.

A WINTER RITUAL: THE YULE CANDLE

For those who do not have a hearth or safe place to burn a log, substitute a brown candle. All the energy and intentions that you would place in a Yule log direct into your candle. The universe, and Spirit, will be just as receptive, and the magic will be just as palpable.

TOOLS YOU WILL NEED:

* ☆ Candle: 1 brown votive or pillar
* ☆ Fireproof plate

* ☆ Herbs: pine, holly, bay leaves, or mistletoe
* ☆ Matches or lighter

1. On the evening of the winter solstice, hold the candle in your hands and bless it with your intentions.
2. Place it on a fireproof plate, arranging the winter herbs around it.
3. Light the candle. By doing so, you are welcoming back the season of light, and manifesting blessings for the coming new year.

A WINTER RITUAL: CLEANSING

Winter solstice is the perfect time to wash away the dark season and welcome in the light with a ritual cleansing of your space, yourself, and your life. What do you need to clean up in order to go forward unfettered in the new year? You can use a variety of herbs and methods for this type of magical cleansing.

To begin, set your intention for this magical cleansing, focusing on exactly what change you need to manifest and bring afresh to your life. These spells will bring magical insight to your winter rituals.

Do you need to see a situation clearly? This spell will help encourage such clarity within your question or issue at hand.

TOOLS YOU WILL NEED:

* ☆ A bottle of white vinegar
* ☆ Spray bottle

* ☆ Herbs: eyebright and angelica

continued →

A Winter Ritual: Cleansing *continued*

1. Pour the white vinegar into the spray bottle. Add a pinch of eyebright and angelica to the white vinegar.

2. Wash the windows of your home.

3. By cleansing the glass so you can view the world in sharp detail and color, you will see the solution or reality of a situation clearly.

Do you need to remove the negative energy of an individual, or a past relationship, in order to move forward productively? This spell will help clear away that detrimental energy.

TOOLS YOU WILL NEED:

* Vacuum
* Pail and mop
* Herbs: rosemary

1. Vacuum your floors, lifting the first layer of dirt, and as you do so, let the first layer of negativity, sadness, or regret be sucked up as well.

2. Next, scrub the floors. Before beginning, add a nice handful of rosemary to the water in your mop bucket. As you scrub the floor, feel yourself washing away the deeply hidden feelings and resentful emotions weighing you down.

3. When you've finished this task, take the bucket of dirty mop water out to the alley, backyard, or green space, and give it a hearty toss over the back fence and say:

   "Be gone!"

Are you having trouble sleeping? Are nightmares and anxiety plaguing you in the dark hours? This spell will soothe that anxiousness and let in the light.

TOOLS YOU WILL NEED:

- ☆ Washing machine and dryer
- ☆ Herbs: dried catnip and comfrey
- ☆ Sage spray

1. Gather all your bedding.
2. Throw it in the washing machine, to which you're going to add a pinch of catnip and comfrey.
3. When it's all clean and dry and you're ready to make up the bed, spray the mattress with sage before you do so.
4. As you make up your bed, recite the mantra:

   "As I sleep upon this bed,
   Pleasant sleep with sweet dreams
   fill my head."

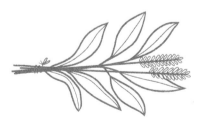

YULE
IMBOLC
OSTARA
BELTANE
LITHA
LUGHNASADH
MABON
SAMHAIN

Slowly Turns the Wheel

The Wheel of the Year is a phrase brought into beautiful illustration and one that Pagans use to mark the seasonal progression throughout all 12 calendar months. This yearly journey encompasses all the energies of holidays, equinoxes and solstices, moon cycles, and seasonal transitions. This annual cycle of seasonal festivals, solar events, and midway points lays at the heart of many a Pagan's spiritual practice.

There are eight Pagan holidays (or Sabbats), with many celebrated worldwide by a variety of cultures and spiritual paths, but often under different names. Where does the Pagan year begin? Of course, the wheel is a circle, making it difficult to tell where it begins and ends. Depending upon an individual's practice and perception, some see the year beginning on October 31 with Samhain (or Halloween), while others believe it falls on or just after the winter solstice (Yule), the one that most closely coincides with our modern mainstream calendar.

For the green witch, the energies of these magical milestones are tied to many a long family tradition filled with expectation, anticipation, excitement, good food, and lots of love. All are worthy of celebration, observation, and honoring in your own green way.

The Sabbats

The dates of the sabbats will vary depending on which hemisphere you live. Differences between the hemispheres are based on the six-month difference in seasons. For example, when it's summer in the Northern Hemisphere, it's winter in the Southern Hemisphere.

YULE: Also known as the winter solstice, Yule is a celebration rejoicing in the return of the sun and the anticipation of the warmth and light it will bring.

IMBOLC: Also known as Candlemas, Imbolc celebrates the transformation of the Old Woman of Winter into the Young Maiden of Spring.

OSTARA: Also known as the spring equinox, Ostara celebrates fertility, rebirth, and renewal. Eggs and the hare are popular symbols for this celebration heralding the time of planting and sowing of seeds.

BELTANE: Also known as May Day, Beltane celebrates human sexuality and fertility, which is personified in the symbols of the maypole and the flowing streams of colorful ribbons.

continued →

Slowly Turns the Wheel *continued*

LITHA: Also known as summer solstice, Litha celebrates the marriage of heaven and earth and new beginnings, which may be one reason that this time of year is so popular for weddings.

LUGHNASADH: Also known as Lammas, this is the first harvest festival celebrating the Earth's bounty, which focuses on wheat, bread being incorporated into the festivities. "May you eat the bread of life."

MABON: Also known as the autumnal equinox, this is the second harvest festival celebrating a successful growing season. This holiday also symbolically puts to rest the growing period, personified by the burning of a Wicker Man filled with vegetation.

SAMHAIN: Also known as Halloween, Samhain celebrates our ancestors, and in many Pagan homes you'll find a special altar filled with photos and mementos of loved ones who have passed.

What are some ways you celebrate the Sabbats and observe the Wheel's cycles?

_____

_____

_____

_____

_____

_____

_____

WATCH CLOSELY YE WEATHER

As with every other aspect of nature and the natural way, the green witch can cast spells that alter the Earth's weather. This is done mostly for protection, or to enhance nature's growth and bounty for gardens and farms. There are dire warnings about weather magic among most practitioners because after all, when we mess with the weather, we're not only affecting our lives, we're also touching many other individuals' paths as well. Keep these thoughts in mind as you connect with the energy, the power, and the magic of the elements and always focus upon positive weather work.

HUSH YE HURRICANE:
A SPELL TO EASE STORMS AND HURRICANES

Both storms and hurricanes contain incredible force and strength. The main culprit in a hurricane and tornado is the wind, of course. With this magic, we'll cast a spell to encourage the extinguishing of this destructive force.

TOOLS YOU WILL NEED:

- Candles: blue, for a hurricane; green, for a tornado (the type of candle you choose—votive, tealight, taper, or pillar—is a personal choice)
- Essential oil: lavender or lemongrass
- Herbs: lavender, anise, and marjoram
- A large gallon jar
- Matches or lighter

1. On the eve of a storm, as soon as you smell it in the air or the warnings start coming through for your area, gather the ingredients for this spell and take them out beneath the sky, whether in a clearing near a wilderness area or in the center of your backyard.

2. On your knees, connected to the ground, pour a few drops of lavender oil on your spell candle and press the herbs onto its sides with both hands. Set this candle in the jar to protect it from the wind and light it.

continued →

3. While this candle burns, close your eyes and turn your face to the sky, feel the breeze, or the drops of rain, and the hardness of the ground beneath your body. Breathe in deeply, smell the rain, fresh air, the damp earth, and the promise of a storm to come.

4. When you feel at one with the energy around you and with the storm itself, open your eyes. Bend forward and blow out the candle's flame. So mote it be.

PERSONAL PROPERTY PROTECTION: A WITCH'S BOTTLE FOR STORM PROTECTION

TOOLS YOU WILL NEED:

- ☆ A small glass jar or bottle
- ☆ Herbs, dried: bay, calamus, fennel, garlic, sage, hyssop, and rosemary
- ☆ Stones: black onyx, tiger's eye, and hematite
- ☆ Essential oil: eucalyptus
- ☆ Cemetery dirt
- ☆ Sea salt
- ☆ Candles: 1 black taper
- ☆ Matches or lighter

1. In your jar or bottle, place the herbs, followed by a generous sprinkling of eucalyptus oil.

2. Anoint each of the stones with this oil and add them to the bottle.

3. Sprinkle in the cemetery dirt and sea salt.

4. Screw the lid securely on your jar or bottle.

5. Light the black candle. Seal the jar with the dripping wax from this candle by carefully picking up the jar in one hand and the candle in the other. Hold the dripping candle at a tilted angle, allowing the wax to drip in a circle around the edges of the lid, generously, as to form a seal. It's perfectly okay for the wax to run over the jar; it's quite all right if you find this process a little messy. The magic is in the brewing and the intention.

6. When the bottle has been created and the wax has cooled and become solid, take this bottle to the northern edge of your property and bury it just within your property line. You can throw a handful of sage and sea salt into this open hole as well. When it's well covered, you can mark this spot with a large stone. If you are an apartment dweller, or are living where this option is just not available to you, take this bottle to a crossroads, where two or more roads intersect, and bury it there.

DRINK DEEP THE EARTH: SPELLS TO END SEASONAL DROUGHT

The following suggestions are quick spells that are derived from old folk magic and can be used to bring rain and end a dry spell.

Place a blue bowl upon the ground. Place a variety of the herbs heather, cardamom, orris, and skullcap in this bowl and fill it with water.

Bathe your cat with magical intention, adding to its bath water a pinch of the herbs licorice and thyme.

Fill a sieve or mesh strainer with hemp, foxglove, myrrh, yarrow, and rose. Hold it above the parched earth and pour water through it.

Fill a mojo bag (a small flannel bag), with a blue lace agate, catnip, and the seeds from cat's tail grass. Toss this bag into a rushing stream.

The cycle of rain and drought are as old as the Earth. Be careful of the energy that comes with calling in rain. Drought often brings panic, and with it frantic prayers for rain from the multitudes and from a variety of spiritual paths. The results? The energy is so concentrated, so powerful, and yet so scattered and undirected, that the result is often floods.

SURGE ON THE SNOW:
A SPELL TO BRING ON SNOWFALL

TOOLS YOU WILL NEED:

⁕ Ice cube tray

⁕ Herbs: mistletoe, holly berries, mint, and marjoram

⁕ Essential oil: peppermint

1. At the beginning of a waxing moon, fill an ice cube tray with water, the herbs, and several generous sprinkles of peppermint oil.

2. Allow the tray to sit undisturbed in your freezer until the evening of a waxing gibbous moon (the midway point to the full moon).

3. When ready, take these ice cubes and grind them in a blender. Take them outside, into your yard and pour some of the crystals into each of the four corners of your property.

FEATHERS AND FLAKES

Feathers are sacred, and their magic is mystical.
With this spell, you'll use their energy and power to bring snowfall.

TOOLS YOU WILL NEED:

⁕ A white feather pillow

⁕ A dagger or pocketknife

1. On a windy, dark winter night during the waxing moon, wrap yourself in a warm cloak and wait until the night is deep and the wind is steady.

2. Either in the center of a crossroads, in a grove of trees, or in the middle of your own backyard, take the pillow and the dagger to this spot.

3. Close your eyes, embrace the cold wind on your face, raise the dagger, and tear an opening in the pillow. Allow the feathers, white and numerous, to scatter in the wind.

4. Stand and ground yourself. Only when you feel ready, retreat to the warmth of your hearth.

FILL THE GREEN HEART: A SPELL TO WELCOME RAINS AND TRANSFORMATIONS

When spring returns, and with it the rains, we will use the energy in celebration to wash away those things we need to cleanse ourselves from. We will also use the refreshing renewable energy of the rain to plant and grow those things that will make our lives flourish. Cast this spell on a brisk sunny day, when you can feel warmth in the air and the growing season descending. Find a spot in your garden, or use flowerpots on your patio or balcony, to pave the way for cleansing and growth.

THE TOOLS YOU WILL NEED:

- ✷ A large stone
- ✷ Black marker
- ✷ Flowerpot
- ✷ Pen and paper

- ✷ Potting soil
- ✷ Flower seeds: zinnias, pansies, marigolds, or a favorite flower of your choice

1. Take a large stone in the palm of your hand. Close your eyes and reflect mindfully upon what it is you need to remove from your life.

2. Whatever comes to the front of your mind, write the name of this person, circumstance, item, habit, or emotion upon the rock using the black marker.

3. Place this stone in the bottom of a flowerpot, or in a carefully dug hole in the garden.

4. On a small strip of paper, write what it is you want to manifest in your life to improve its quality.

5. Place this strip of paper on top of the large stone.

6. Add several handfuls of garden soil (or potting soil, if you're using flowerpots). When the rock and the paper is almost covered, but not quite, add a pinch of zinnia seeds and then lightly cover them.

GREET YE SUN: A SPELL TO THANK THE SUN

One of the ways the green witch has of celebrating, honoring, and giving thanks to something, is to set up an altar. This altar can be large and take up the top of a dining room table, or it can be a small space relegated to a windowsill or the corner of a bookshelf.

You can set up this altar for some long-term magic, or you can set it up for a weekend and a concentrated dose of sun-sation. You can light candles daily, burn incense, or add fresh herbs periodically, or you can set everything up at once, lighting what needs to be lit, and spend the rest of the time admiring your creation as you pass by this magical spot.

TOOLS YOU WILL NEED:

- ⚹ Table or shelf
- ⚹ Candles: yellow and gold votives
- ⚹ Stones: sunstone, tiger's eye, yellow topaz, carnelian, amber, citrine
- ⚹ Herbs: fresh if possible, dried if not: marigold, heliotrope, sunflower, buttercup, cedar, beech, oak, St. John's wort, bergamot, sandalwood, angelica, bay, rosemary, frankincense, ginseng, juniper, and goldenseal
- ⚹ Incense: sandalwood, bergamot, juniper, and frankincense
- ⚹ Matches or lighter

1. Clear a space for your altar, whether this is a special table, a windowsill, or an outdoor area.

2. Place your candles on your altar and arrange the stones around them.

3. Add the herbs to your altar, making sure they're a safe distance from the candles.

4. Light your candles and incense.

5. Tend your altar carefully, whether daily for a limited time, or whether you plan to keep this altar up for a while. Change out the candles and herbs and incense as needed. Remember not to leave burning candles unattended.

Phases of the Moon and Esbats

Waxing Moon
The energy of the waxing moon is used for attraction, to draw something to you.

Waning Moon
The energy of the waning moon is used to banish, to send something away from you.

Full Moon
The energy of the full moon is considered the most potent time to harness the moon's vibrations for magical purposes.

New Moon
This moon energy is often used for divination, for magic steeped in mysticism and clairvoyance.

Esbats

Oak Moon (December)
The oak moon is all about reflection on what it is that you want to keep in your life and those things that should be removed.

Wolf Moon (January)
January will be a time to bury the hatchet, to shake hands and reconnect. Communication and the energies connected to it are potent this time of year, and communication is key with the wolf moon.

Storm Moon (February)
This energy is connected to spirituality and the crown chakra. Many will use the energy of the storm moon to reach a new level of enlightenment.

Hare Moon (March)
The no-nonsense energy of March's moon is the perfect energy in which to cast spells to free a voice that's been silent too long.

Seed Moon (April)
The seed moon heralds a time of fertility and a manifestation of physical desires. Garden magic and planting is powerful at this time.

Dryad Moon (May)
The heart chakra is emphasized, and with it a whole list of emotional issues that you can work on connected to love, friendships, relationships, and emotions.

Mead Moon (June)
Cast spells now to honor and strengthen the ego, along with self-confidence, to prepare yourself for future endeavors and challenges.

Herb Moon (July)
Harness the magic of the herb moon to enhance your personal power, your leadership abilities, your resolve, and determination.

Barley Moon (August)
The barley moon lends its energy to a pre-winter cleansing that includes not only our physical environment, but emotional cleansing as well.

Harvest Moon (September)
If you have legal issues coming up, cast a spell for positive judicial magic to manifest in the mundane realm. It's all about justice.

Hunter's Moon (October)
This month and its energy lend itself well for spells that remove blocks, rituals that clear our path for positive forward movement.

Snow Moon (November)
The snow moon will lend its energy to release something in our lives, bringing much-needed relief and emancipation.

NOTES AND REFLECTIONS

NOTES AND REFLECTIONS

CHAPTER 2

Of Stones & Wax: Magic with Crystals, Candles & Incense

Welcome to the world of candle magic, crystal energy, and the ability to align specific intentions with the pungent aroma of incense. All three of these ingredients add up to a spell-casting experience that is powerful, successful, and spiritually uplifting. Read ahead to expand your practice by learning how to incorporate this magic into your life.

CLEANSING AND CHARGING YOUR CRYSTALS

Crystals and stones pick up and retain energy, whether from individuals handling them in a store, or the energy of a magical ritual or spell in which they were used. Your crystals should be cleansed periodically to eliminate and clear any residual energy they've acquired, and absolutely need to be cleansed between magical uses.

You can cleanse your crystals by using any of the following:

Natural light: leaving them to bathe in the moonlight, or sunlight, for a period of time, depending upon which energy aligns with you

Smudging: holding them in the smoke of incense, such as sandalwood, which is excellent for cleansing and purification, or sage, a timeless and time-honored herb used for cleansing just about anything

By touch: holding them in the palm of your hand, using them during meditation to enhance your experience and deepen your bond with the stone, as well as aligning the stone with specific intentions at the same time

With water: holding them under running water, either natural running water like a stream, or your kitchen faucet, both of which will do the job

CRYSTAL CLEAR SPELLS AND MEDITATIONS

Crystals have long been used in magical practices to manifest desires, to draw something in (or send something away), to strengthen our intentions for a spell, to protect us, to lend their energy for healing, and any number of other purposes to enhance our life. The energy of crystals is inherent within the stone itself. All we have to do is learn how to tap into this magical resource.

AMETHYST MEDITATION

Amethyst crystals are connected to the crown chakra and an amplified sense of spirituality, as in connecting on a personal level with divinity and spiritual enlightenment. This stone is also excellent for healing purposes, for fighting addictions, as well as for finding clarity within ourselves and our personal circumstances leading to the resolution of issues, or a new perspective that makes acceptance easier.

TOOLS YOU WILL NEED:

☆ Candles: 4 purple pillars

☆ Stones: 4 amethyst crystals to set with the candles and one amethyst crystal to fit in your hand

☆ Matches or lighter

☆ Soft pillow and blanket (optional)

1. Create a sacred space by placing four purple pillar candles at the four directions, with an amethyst crystal in the space between each candle. You'll also want your favorite amethyst crystal to hold in your hand. Sit in the center and get comfortable. For some of us, this includes soft pillows and maybe a blanket. When the body is cozy and safe, it's easier for the spirit to attend to greater things.

2. Once settled, clear your mind. Visualize a large, purple wooden door in the wall of a sage-green stone cottage. The door is bordered with green ivy, the air is warm and moist and still, and there may be a white cat sitting on the stone steps. Allow yourself to sink deeply into this image. Smell the air and appreciate the beauty of the ivy and the way it clings to the wall of the cottage. Watch the cat. Something has caught its attention, and it turns now to the dark purple door.

3. You can see that this door is slowly starting to open, and as it does so, you hear the soft creak of its ancient metal hinges. The cat slips through the first crack, disappearing within, and as the door continues to open . . . follow the cat.

4. Follow this spirit guide through the purple door to the realms of your psyche. Explore the dark corners and secret niches of your inner consciousness and embrace what you find here. Accept the shadows and gray areas in order to learn and grow and heal mentally, spiritually, and emotionally. But also, celebrate the light you find there and walk in joy.

CALMING QUARTZ RITUAL

Clear crystal quartz is a blank slate, easily absorbing your energy and intentions. This stone also adds its energy to and amplifies that of any other stone placed with it, helps you to focus, and to clarify your dreams. We're going to create an altar for meditation and ritual using clear quartz crystals and two other stones of your choice, depending upon what your personal focus and desires might be.

TOOLS YOU WILL NEED:

- ☆ Table
- ☆ Altar cloth
- ☆ Clear quartz crystal point or selenite tower
- ☆ Polished clear quartz crystals
- ☆ Two stones of your choice
- ☆ Candles: 1 white pillar and 4 white votives
- ☆ Incense: a scent of your choice
- ☆ Matches or lighter

1. On your table, spread the cloth of your choice. In the center of the table, place either a flat-bottomed clear quartz crystal point, or a crystal point that can lay on its side, or a flat-bottomed tower crystal of selenite. Another form of selenite crystal will work, whether it's a sphere or a nice simple piece of any size. Selenite is filled with energy and is the stone most used as a generator for crystal grids. Any of these options will make a successful generator for your crystal grid. If you don't have crystal points or selenite in your arsenal of crystals and stones, choose a clear crystal, or a stone that carries your intentions, and use this as the center stone for your grid.

2. Around this center stone, lay a ring of polished clear quartz crystal stones, as many as you feel is right for your intentions. Around the outside of this ring of crystals, place a ring of stones of your own choosing. What is your intention for this grid? Where are your energies focused? If it's on love and relationships, use rose quartz. If you need to clear negative energy and protect yourself from other people's negative thoughts and intentions, try black tourmaline or black onyx. If this crystal grid is being created to heal, or to bring prosperity, use adventurine or moss agates.

3. Set a single white pillar candle on this table and four white votive candles to create the four corners. Choose incense and place this on the table near the crystals. Light your candles and your incense.

4. Hold the index finger of your power hand over the center generating crystal. Hovering above the crystal grid, pull this energy out to one of the clear quartz crystals around it, then back to the generator.

5. Keep this energy moving. From the generator, pull this energy out to the next crystal and back to the generator, going all the way around the circle, from crystal to crystal, in and out, from the generator to each of the crystals around it. You may do this once, or you may continue the motion to build energy. This is the traditional way to activate a crystal grid, and I can tell you from personal experience that you may feel a physical shift in the energy around you.

GARNET MEDITATION AND MOJO BAG

The garnet shields us from negativity and is said to be a protective stone for witches. The garnet also helps us reach a higher expression of love with more focused and purposeful energy. To carry the magic of the garnet with you as you go through the day's journey, we're going to make a mojo bag to carry in our pockets, our purses, in our vehicles, or to place in a subtle spot in our desk or work area.

TOOLS YOU WILL NEED:

- A small bag: colorful gauze or velvet (either purchased or handmade)
- Stones: several small, polished garnet stones
- Herbs: whole allspice, powdered cumin, and dried wormwood
- Incense: dragon's blood or patchouli
- Matches or lighter

1. Cleanse the garnet stones under running water. Add them to your gauze or velvet bag. Add a pinch of whole allspice, cumin, and wormwood to the bag.

2. Light the incense. Tie the bag shut, then hold it in the smoke of your incense to cleanse and consecrate it. Consider cleansing this bag every so often, maybe once a month, to keep the energy clear and flowing.

MOON MAGIC MOONSTONE RITUAL

Moonstone is noted for its fine-tuned connection with all things feminine, including divinity, spirituality, and the cycles of womanhood. This stone is closely associated with keen intuition, clairvoyance, empathic energies, and

continued →

Moon Magic Moonstone Ritual *continued*

everything that goes with the gift of second sight. Its energy and planetary connection are aligned with, of course, the moon. To embrace the powerful energies that go with this stone, you'll consecrate an amulet that you can wear to provide you with a never-ending connection.

TOOLS YOU WILL NEED:

- ⚝ Moonstone pendant
- ⚝ Soft cloth
- ⚝ Candle: 1 white votive
- ⚝ Incense: gardenia, jasmine, or myrrh
- ⚝ Matches or lighter
- ⚝ Silver chain

1. Shop for your moonstone pendant at your local new-age, jewelry, or rock shop, or shop online. When you find the pendant that speaks to you, you'll know without a doubt. Take this pendant home and get it ready for consecration.

2. First, place it under running water to wash away any residual energy it may have picked up along the way. Dry it with a soft cloth.

3. Light your candle and your incense. Place your pendant on a silver chain and hold it in the smoke of the incense as you consecrate it, saying:

    "By the power of the moon,

    May its gifts reside

    within this stone.

    That I may walk with Spirit

    and not alone."

Evoking the Energies

The seven energies central to the green witch and our magical practice are paramount to a well-rounded spirituality. These are energies that make our lives run more smoothly, make our existence meaningful, and bring great fulfillment to everyone who is touched by this magic. To invoke these energies, use the following candles, herbs, incense, and stones to empower your work.

Abundance: brown candles, mint and goldenrod, incense of cinnamon, magnets and stones of adventurine

Happiness: yellow candles, sunflowers and calendula, incense of patchouli, stones of yellow calcite and citrine

Harmony: candles in shades of blue, violets and lilacs, incense of lavender, blue azurite and lapis stones

Health: candles in shades of green, St John's wort and goldenseal, incense of lemongrass, blue lace agate stones

Love: red and pink candles, rose blossoms and red geraniums, incense of jasmine, rose quartz and morganite stones

Peace: pink and white candles, lily of the valley and chamomile, incense of primrose and lavender, rhodocrosite and charoite stones

Protection: black candles, allspice and cinnamon and garlic, incense of dragon's blood, black stones of obsidian and tourmaline

A RAINBOW OF CANDLES

Colors are also significant for magical correspondences in rituals and spells, and color is especially important when it comes to candle magic. Immerse yourself in the range of magical possibilities these candles and colors can provide.

Red is for fire and passion, lust and love. It ignites the energy and force needed to see something through, strength and endurance for the long haul.

Black deflects negativity, clears, and cleanses. A black candle will make your space safe again and you along with it.

Green will heal the physical body and the heart. It will also bring in prosperity, drawing money to you.

White is your go-to color for all situations. If you only have a white candle, that's okay; imbue it with your intention and watch magic happen.

Yellow is the color you want to open or clear communication. It will inspire the artist and creative muses.

Blue will help you handle emotional issues. This is also the color you'll need for intuitive and psychic energies, and the color to enhance your second sight.

Purple will handle legal and money issues. This is your color to go to for judicial energy, as well as for business and finance.

Orange will lend its vibrant power when you need to fight a battle.

CANDLE MAGIC

Candle magic is popular and powerful. To perform these spells, you will imbue your spell candle with your intentions and a range of other simple tools will help add power and resonance.

BLESSING SPELL

This is the perfect spell to cast when the energy around someone has been feeling slightly "off" or when there's some positive energy needed in someone's life for specific circumstances or conditions.

TOOLS YOU WILL NEED:

- Straight pin
- Candle: 1 white votive
- Essential oil: lavender
- Herbs: frankincense, sandalwood, or wormwood
- Fireproof plate
- Silver coin
- Incense: a scent of your choice
- A small bag of gauze, flannel, or cotton
- Matches or lighter

1. On the day of a waxing moon, sit somewhere quiet where you can contemplate exactly what you wish to manifest.

2. Using the straight pin, inscribe on the candle a single word or name that coincides with what you wish to affect with this spell. Consider inscribing a number linked to a date, or a birthday, or something else connected to your intention.

3. Pour a few drops of lavender oil in the palm of your hand and anoint your candle.

4. Combine the crushed herbs and grind them together until well blended. Pour these herbs out in a line on a smooth surface and, laying your candle on its side, roll it in these herbs until they adhere to the surface.

5. Place your candle on the fireproof plate, with the silver coin beneath it. Light your anointed candle and the incense.

6. Close your eyes. Visualize the outcome of your spell, feeling the overwhelming sensation of peace, comfort, and stability.

7. Open your eyes and light the candle. Allow it to burn down in one sitting, if possible. If this isn't possible, extinguish your candle with a candlesnuffer or small drinking glass; don't blow it out. You can relight it once you're able to do so. The magic will continue undisrupted.

continued →

8. Once your candle is spent, gather whatever its remnants—the wax and herbs and such—and the silver coin, and place them in a small bag.

9. Bury this bag on sacred ground, either in a churchyard or in a cemetery, where the consecrated space will strengthen your connection to Spirit and keep your intentions pure.

SELF-LOVE SPELL

Sometimes as life overwhelms us and we've been exposed to negative people and energy or listened to too much criticism, it's time to reclaim and love ourselves, and celebrate our indomitable spirit. To relearn how to do this, we're going to *bathe with intention*. This ritual may be done in the depths of a warm bath or in the healing waters of a shower.

TOOLS YOU WILL NEED:

- ✳ Bathtub or shower
- ✳ Herbs: rose blossoms, hyacinth, pink geranium blossoms, or a sprig of rosemary
- ✳ Essential oil: rose
- ✳ Candles: 6 pink votives
- ✳ Stones: rose quartz, rhodochrosite, and lepidolite
- ✳ Incense: Nag Champa, rose, or your favorite scent
- ✳ Matches or lighter
- ✳ Small cloth bag of gauze, cotton, or flannel

1. On a quiet evening when you feel your emotional reserves are running low, fill your bathtub with hot water.

2. Add the herbs and rose oil to it.

3. Place the candles and stones around the edge of your tub, or if that's not possible, place them on the floor in front of your tub, alternating the candles and stones.

4. Light the candles and the incense.

5. Slowly, reverently, step into the tub or shower. As you get comfortable, be aware of the movement of energy around you. Feel the power in the charged water, accept the cleansing smoke of the incense, feel the passion of self-love in the candles, and vibrate in harmony with the energy of the stones.

6. When your bathing is done and the candles extinguished, gather the stones and add them to a small bag. To carry forth this self-love, keep them in a safe and secret place; you can carry them in your purse; or keep them on your nightstand, whatever you feel called to do.

HARMONY SPELL

When there is discord in your life, it will touch your life on all levels, often in very subtle and negative ways. What you're going to have to do is to restore balance and harmony. We're going to use this spell to attract harmonic peaceful energy by either exposing these stones to a location connected with discord, or by having an individual with whom you're in discord touch a stone. Either way, the important thing is that these stones are subject to the energy we wish to be rid of.

TOOLS YOU WILL NEED:

⋆ Stones: amethyst, sodalite, and kunzite

⋆ Candle: a green pillar or a seven-day candle

⋆ Essential oil: lilac

⋆ Herbs: chamomile, valerian, skullcap, and meadowsweet (gently crushed before using)

⋆ Matches or lighter

1. Before the waning gibbous moon, take the stones of amethyst, sodalite, and kunzite with you on a journey.

2. Once this has been accomplished, take these stones to a crossroads and bury them.

3. On the evening of the waning gibbous moon, fix your spell candle.

4. Hold it in your hands and imbue it with your desire and intention of harmony and peace. Anoint the candle with lilac oil.

continued →

5. Combine the crushed herbs and grind them together until well blended. Pour these herbs out in a line on a smooth surface and, laying your candle on its side, roll it in these herbs until they adhere to the surface.

6. Light this candle for seven consecutive nights, letting it burn a few minutes each night. On the seventh night, extinguish the candle for the last time.

7. Take whatever remains of this candle and bury it on your property. As an alternative, the remnants from this spell may be buried on consecrated ground, a cemetery, or churchyard, to seal the energy and the spell.

BRAVERY SPELL

Not all of us face daunting danger every day, but sometimes we all face something that scares us. It's okay to be scared but it's not okay to flee in the face of something we need to confront. When something is coming up in life and you're going to need a little extra courage to stand up to it, cast this spell.

TOOLS YOU WILL NEED:

*   Candle: an orange votive
*   Essential oil: dragon's blood
*   Mortar and pestle
*   Herbs: dragon's blood, black cohosh, and thyme
*   Fireproof dish
*   Stones: blood stone, carnelian, and red jasper
*   Matches or lighter

1. On the night of a waxing moon, hold the orange candle in your hands and think about what it is you're afraid of. What are the repercussions of this fear? How will they impact your life? What do you need to feel confident in facing this challenge?

2. Once this is clear in your mind, it's time to ground yourself and connect with earth's energy. Harness this magic, from the soles of your feet, up through your legs. Feel it coursing through the trunk of your body, down your arms, to your hands, and into the candle.

3. Anoint this candle with the dragon's blood oil.

4. Crush the herbs using the mortar and pestle. Combine the crushed herbs and grind them together until well blended. Pour these herbs out in a line on a smooth surface and, laying your candle on its side, roll it in these herbs until they adhere to the surface.

5. Set this candle on a fireproof dish and surround it with the stones.

6. As you light this orange candle, filled with the energy and power of bravery, say:

"As this flame burns bright;

Courage courses through the night.

Into my soul it flows with might;

Bravery comes with morning light."

SWEET DREAMS SPELL

Dreams have always fascinated human beings, and along with the fascination come magical ways of controlling, filtering, or even producing and enhancing them. From the familiar dream catcher used to filter nightmares from positive dreams, to the more mystic use of ritualistic herbs, the means and ways to experience this mysterious inner world has never ceased to inspire us. This spell combines a candle spell and the creation of a mojo bag you can place in a pillowcase to enhance your dreams, while protecting you from nightmares.

TOOLS YOU WILL NEED:

* Candle: 1 yellow votive and 1 black votive
* Essential oil: chamomile
* Fireproof plate
* Herbs: mugwort, chamomile, rosemary, blue vervain, and sage
* Stones
* Incense: lavender
* Matches or lighter
* Small black bag of gauze or velvet

1. On the night before a full moon, sit in a comfortable and private space.

2. Hold the candles in your hands, focusing your intention upon them.

3. When you feel that the energy is right, anoint these candles with chamomile oil and place them in the center of a fireproof plate.

4. Sprinkle the herbs in a circle around the candles, and place your stones around them as well. Light the candles and the incense.

5. Allow these candles to burn out in one sitting.

6. When everything has cooled, add the remnants of this spell to your bag—any remaining cooled candle wax, the herbs, and the stones—and several drops of chamomile oil.

7. Place this mojo bag in your pillowcase. You can keep this bag in your pillowcase to ensure sweet dreams and an absence of nightmares, or you can store this bag in a box under your bed, or in a bureau drawer, and place it in your pillowcase when your sleep is being disrupted by nightmares.

GARDEN GOOD LUCK SPELL

There are so many magical ways to bring luck, from the old-world charm of the rabbit's foot to the four-leaf clover and the iron horseshoe. We are always looking for new ways to change our luck, or to draw good luck to us, and that's exactly what we're going to do with this spell. You're going to use the natural energy of your garden, along with a magical garden stepping-stone, to bring in a constant flow of positive, lucky energy. If you don't have access to a garden spot, you can use the river stone listed in the tools list on page XII. You can keep this stone and its magic close to you by keeping it in a flowerpot buried beneath the soil.

TOOLS YOU WILL NEED:

- ✳ A garden stepping-stone
- ✳ Herbs: calamus, star anise, and one whole nutmeg
- ✳ Stone: pyrite
- ✳ Candle: 1 white votive
- ✳ Matches or lighter

1. On a beautiful, still day when your garden or chosen green space naturally calls to you, choose a spot for your stepping-stone, either in a quiet, unobtrusive corner or at an entrance where you'll step over it often.

2. At this spot, dig a small hole and toss into it the herbs and the pyrite.

3. Place your large stepping-stone in its resting place.

4. Set the tea candle in the center of this stone and light it. As you light the candle, say:

   "By the vision of this flame I see,

   Good luck flows to me.

   Through the energy and its tone,

   Good luck is set in stone."

PROTECTION FROM JEALOUSY AND SPITE

Thoughts are energy, whether they are happy, positive thoughts or negative and possibly harmful thoughts. This candle spell will shield, repel, and protect you from other people's harmful thoughts of jealousy and spite, two of the most common and most destructive emotions and energies.

TOOLS YOU WILL NEED:

- ☆ Candle: 1 black votive
- ☆ Essential oil: sage
- ☆ Herbs: cloves, allspice, cayenne pepper, and garlic (ground)
- ☆ Three thorns from a rose bush
- ☆ Red brick
- ☆ Incense: cinnamon
- ☆ Matches or lighter
- ☆ Small black bag of gauze or velvet

1. On the night of a waning gibbous moon, in a place that feels comfortable and safe and private for you, anoint the candle with the oil and the herbs. Take each of the three thorns in turn and pierce the candle; as you do so, say:

   "Thorn of one,
   It is done.

   Thorn of two,
   You are through.

   Thorn of three,
   You can't touch me."

2. Place this candle on the red brick and light it and the incense.

3. When the candle has burned down, take any of the remnants, including the remains of the wax and the thorns, place them in a small black bag, and bury it in the dead of night at a crossroads in the country, in the still of the night beneath a tree in a park or in a corner of a deserted city lot.

What are some other ways you disperse negative feelings and emotions using your magic?

_____

_____

TRUTH SPELLS

How insidious is a lie, and how awful is the sense of betrayal when we've fallen victim to a falsehood. Then there are times when the truth is elusive or more difficult to define. These are spells to reveal a lie, to unravel the truth, and to discern the source.

MELT THE LIAR

Unfortunately, we encounter liars in everyday life. We don't have to feel like a victim when we fall for their falsehoods. We have the power to find out who they are to avoid them or keep them away from the people in our lives. This spell will help reveal the identity of a liar.

TOOLS YOU WILL NEED:

- ☆ Ice cube tray
- ☆ Water
- ☆ Pen and paper

1. When the culprit of a lie that you or a close friend have fallen victim to is not clearly identified, fill an ice cube tray with water.

2. Write the names of the individuals you suspect of falsehood on small pieces of paper and fold and place them in the bottom of the tray, one slip of paper for every individual you suspect of lying to you.

3. After the ice cubes are frozen, remove the pieces of paper from the tray and lay them in the light of a full moon. The last ice cube to melt completely will contain the name of the guilty party.

LOOSEN THE TONGUE

Sometimes you want the liars you encounter to stop telling falsehoods and just tell the truth. It isn't easy to convince people that the truth will set them free. This spell will help you loosen their tongues a bit.

TOOLS YOU WILL NEED:

* Red, white, and black sewing thread, approximately 12 inches in length each
* Small piece of paper and pen
* White envelope
* Matches or lighter

1. Gather the loose sewing threads of red, white, and black.

2. Roll, tangle, and mix them up.

3. Write the name of the liar on a small slip of paper and put it with these threads in a white envelope.

4. Set fire to this incriminating package and disperse the ashes to the wind. As the ashes blow free, so does the tongue of the one who lies.

A SPELL FOR SAFE TRAVELS

When you find yourself on the road, packing your bags for a monumental journey, you may want some extra magical protection. When my children were small, before a car trip I'd roll up my sleeves for a magical ritual in our driveway, much to our neighbors' consternation. This is a spell for some added protection and peace of mind, whether you're driving cross-country or a daily commute. If you like, take a snippet of hair given voluntarily from the driver as well as people who are regular passengers and add it to the mojo bag, giving this protection spell a uniquely personal twist. Happy trails!

TOOLS YOU WILL NEED:

* Candles: green, yellow, red, and blue (for each of the four elements)
* Incense: sandalwood
* Matches or lighter
* Sage smudge stick
* Essential oil: Mars astrological oil (page 69) or rosemary and sandalwood oils
* Stones: tiger's eye, turquoise, and dalmatian jasper

☆ **Small cloth bag of gauze,
cotton, or flannel**

☆ **Sea salt**

☆ **Herbs: calamus root and plantain**

1. Place the candles on the ground around the vehicle you'll be traveling in, at the four directions, lighting them and the incense.

2. Open all the doors on the vehicle and proceed to smudge the inside with a lit stick of sage, working your way around the vehicle, stopping at each open door and leaning inside.

3. Take the Mars astrological oil and anoint the vehicle on all four sides, at the center of each side.

4. Anoint all the doors.

5. Anoint each one of the stones when you have finished with the vehicle.

6. Create a mojo bag by adding the three stones, the sea salt, the calamus root, and plantain to the small cloth bag.

7. Hang this bag from the rearview mirror or keep it in the glove compartment or tucked under the driver's seat.

Note: You may not always be traveling in your own vehicle, or even with the same mode of transportation every day. If you take public transportation, you naturally won't be able to perform the full spell for safe travels. However, you can still add a measure of this spell to any mode of transportation you'll be using by anointing a stone of tiger's eye with Mars astrological oil and carrying it in your purse or pocket.

INCENSE AND SMUDGING

Before the green witch begins a ritual or casting a spell, they will cleanse their space with the smoke from incense or herbs. This is an age-old practice from many cultures and spiritual paths called "smudging."

CLEANSING

Cleansing is a time-honored witch's ritual to clear your living space of negative energy or unwanted entities by using smoke from herbs or incense. The terms "saging" and "smudging" are often used interchangeably for this process. You will often notice the aftereffects of routinely cleansing your home as a feeling of "lightness" (both physically and mentally), a more relaxed atmosphere in general, and a good night's sleep will often be easier to achieve.

TOOLS YOU WILL NEED:

- ✶ Candles: 1 white pillar
- ✶ Essential oil: sandalwood oil
- ✶ Incense: sandalwood
- ✶ Sage smudge stick
- ✶ Feather: a raven's feather is preferred, but a more common feather will work
- ✶ Abalone shell or fireproof plate (optional)

1. Anoint the white pillar candle with sandalwood oil. Place it in the center of your home, perhaps on the ground floor in the living room, and light it with the incense. As an alternative, if you have help with this ritual, have someone carry this candle from room to room as you go.

2. Light the sage bundle, and beginning on the lowest level of your abode, go from room to room, circling each room clockwise as you go, holding the lit sage bundle in one hand and the feather in the other. Using the feather to gently waft the smoke rising from the sage, disperse it to the four corners of each room. Don't forget closets or nooks and crannies.

3. Work your way through your home, down the hallways, up flights of stairs, spreading the sage smoke with the feather as you go. You can speak your intentions while performing this ritual:

"With this sage, Be gone bad things,
With this sage, And raven's wings."

ENERGIZING

You can use a favorite incense to add a specific energy to a space for a number of reasons. It's always helpful to light incense in a space before a large gathering, a meeting between friends, or before a date. Before a social gathering, you may want to do a smudging with sage to cleanse the space generally of any residual energy. See the first ritual (page 52) for cleansing. Once you've cleansed the space by smudging, you'll want to set the energy with this ritual before your guests arrive.

TOOLS YOU WILL NEED:

- ✶ Sage smudge stick
- ✶ Vacuum or broom (optional)
- ✶ Herbs: sweet grass
- ✶ Candle: 1 white votive candle

- ✶ Incense: lavender and rose
- ✶ Matches or lighter
- ✶ Glasses or goblets
- ✶ A libation of your choice

1. Make sure that the area where you'll be entertaining your guests is physically clean and tidy, minus any unnecessary clutter, dirty dishes, or dust bunnies. Vacuum or sweep the floor, as heavier energy tends to settle here.

2. Before company comes, light your sweet grass and disperse this smoke throughout the area where you'll be entertaining your guests.

3. Set your candle and incense on the dining room table, a coffee table, or an end table and light it. It's nice to have this out in the open, as it's pretty and sets a certain ambient mood. People tend to relax around candles and incense.

4. Once your guests arrive, get your refreshments ready: Pour your beverages and get ready to share some lively conversation and magical connections.

BLESSING

When purchasing new stones or a new piece of magical jewelry, it's always nice to smudge it, cleansing it of scattered energies it may have picked up along its journey as well as bestowing a blessing upon it, often for particular intentions. Blessing your amulet can be as ritualistic, or as informal, as you wish. This blessing can be conducted in the sacred space of a cast circle, if you feel the need.

TOOLS YOU WILL NEED:

- Candle: 1 black votive
- Amulet: a design of your choice
- Essential oil: dragon's blood
- Incense: dragon's blood
- Matches or lighter

To create an amulet for protection: Light your black candle and dragon's blood incense, anoint your amulet with dragon's blood oil, and while it's encased in the warmth of your hands and bathed in the magical scent, set your intentions for this piece of jewelry as a form of powerful protection. Then hold the amulet in the smoke of the incense while saying:

"May this amulet protect me
From malice and negativity.
Guard me with the four elements,
Guard me from the four directions,
Guard me with magic from above,
Guard me from below.
Guard me by the morning tide,
Guard me by the evening flow."

CENTERING BEFORE RITUAL WORK

Before casting your circle and beginning any magical endeavor, you will need to ground and center yourself. You'll need to still the everyday mundane chatter in your mind, need to connect to other energies the universe offers to us for our spiritual enlightenment and success. You may use incense and smudging as part of this grounding process. Be sure to do this in a comfortable place, preferably on the floor or ground.

TOOLS YOU WILL NEED:

- ☆ Candle: 1 purple pillar
- ☆ Essential oil: copal or frankincense
- ☆ Fireproof plate
- ☆ Stones: smoky quartz and hematite
- ☆ Incense: copal or frankincense
- ☆ Matches or lighter

1. Anoint the candle with the essential oil and place it on a fireproof plate. Around this candle, arrange the stones and light the incense.

2. Now comes the difficult part for most people. Your brain has a constant stream of conversation and consciousnesses running through it, whether you're always aware of it or not. It takes some concentration and practice to still this mind chatter so that more subtle energy, wisps of second sight, and power for magical purposes can be brought into focus.

3. Hear the stillness in order to proceed with your rituals or spell crafting. Once you've accomplished this, the small subconscious voice inside your head will take on new depth and volume.

4. You may see visions that are coming to you from somewhere that is not you; you may literally hear a voice, either internally, or physically with your ears. You may see flashes of people who have passed, and you might experience other sensations that you will realize are not of your own creation. Some people experience a feeling of revelation and spiritual enlightenment.

BANISHING NEGATIVE INFLUENCES AND THOUGHTS

How hard is it to stop thinking about some slight we've received or a betrayal (real or imagined)? How hard is it to silence that nasty little voice in our head giving us terrible advice? It's incredibly difficult to escape these very human emotions and thought patterns, and not being able to control these things can put our happiness in jeopardy. This spell will help slough off those influences.

TOOLS YOU WILL NEED:

- ✯ Candle: 1 black votive
- ✯ Essential oil: cinnamon or cedar
- ✯ Fireproof plate
- ✯ Stones: black onyx, apache tears, black obsidian, and tourmaline
- ✯ Incense: cinnamon
- ✯ Matches or lighter
- ✯ Pen and paper
- ✯ Small cloth bag of gauze, cotton, or flannel
- ✯ A thumbtack
- ✯ Thorns from a rosebush

1. Cast your circle.

2. Anoint your candle with the oil, placing it in the center of the fireproof plate.

3. Place your stones and herbs around the candle in an arrangement that is positive for you.

4. Light the candle and the incense.

5. Sit and pick up the pen and paper. Tearing the paper into small squares, write one of the demons that plagues your mind upon each piece.

6. As you write down each one, hold this small square of paper over the candle flame and ignite it, allowing it to burn to ash.

7. When all is done and the candle has cooled, gather everything on the plate and place it in the cloth bag, along with the thumbtack and thorns.

8. Anoint this bag with one of the essential oils and bury it off your property, such as in a ditch along a quiet country road, in the corner of an abandoned city lot, or toss the bag into your nearest trash can.

NOTES AND REFLECTIONS

NOTES AND REFLECTIONS

NOTES AND REFLECTIONS

CHAPTER 3

Within Your Witchy Kitchen: Magical Remedies & Recipes

In this chapter, we'll be covering the essentials for the green witch's kitchen, ensuring you'll have all the tools you'll need to create your balms, salves, oils, tinctures, and elixirs. With the help of this grimoire, you'll soon learn how to empower a balm, craft a magical tea, and bake a cake or cookies for ritual ceremonial use.

continued →

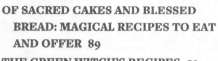

THE WITCH'S KITCHEN

The following supplies will be needed to successfully create the magical recipes that follow in these pages.

Saucepans and pots: Should budgets and space allow, you'll find a variety of pot sizes useful, from very small saucepans to more cauldron-like pots and kettles. You may also want a double set, so one set can be used for special ceremonial or ritual recipes. Considering the reverence and magical energy involved in the ritual preparation of foods, teas, and potions, it is considered good spiritual etiquette to use a separate set of pots and pans and utensils for this purpose. Occasionally, there may be some ingredients used that are not edible, or appealing, to prepare with utensils used for normal meal preparation.

Teapot: A small teapot is for heating water, or a large teakettle.

Strainer: A small strainer will be needed to strain herbs from liquids.

Spoons: Spoons in several sizes for stirring and mixing, as well as a set of measuring spoons, will come in handy when assembling your magical recipes.

Glass bottles: To store your magical creations, you'll need glass bottles in a variety of sizes, shapes, and styles, both with screw-top lids as well as corks.

Twine: Among other purposes, use it to tie labeling tags to your bottles.

Ceramic cups and bowls: You will most likely collect a variety of colorful teacups and bowls that you will use to sip your ritual teas, as well as to blend herbs and ingredients. Many green witches develop quite a penchant for these pretty, useful utensils, and our cupboards can attest to the joys of collecting such items.

Mortar and pestle: Some of the herbs and ingredients you'll be using will need to be thoroughly ground and blended, and you will find mortar and pestle indispensable for this. Grinding ingredients by hand also brings you closer to their natural scents and essences, enriching your magical experience.

Eye dropper: These are always handy when you need to add a drop of this or that to a magical recipe.

Fabric bags: You'll use a variety of bags in different sizes and colors, and in different fabrics, both gauze and transparent, heavier velvet, as well as light cotton.

THE WITCH'S GARDEN

Whether you live in the garden-ready country or you're a city dweller who tends to your balcony's potted plants you'll find a way to grow, tend, and harvest the herbs you need. The following list is just a few of the herbs you will find essential.

 Aloe: For protection and luck. Aloe guards against evil influences, whether physical or influential energy, and protects your home.

 Basil: For love and prosperity. Use basil in a ritual bath to bring new love to you or to wash away the residual and lingering energy of an old love.

 Catnip: For love and beauty. Burn catnip to manifest wishes. Drink tea for relaxation, meditation, and to connect you with your totem animal.

 Cayenne pepper: For love and uncrossing. Add this herb to any magical working that needs to be spiced up and loaded with passion.

 Chile pepper: For love and good luck. Use this in love spells to ensure that the passion remains spicy and hot. Use its fiery potency as well to break a string of bad luck.

 Cinnamon: For love, lust, healing, psychic powers, protection, and money drawing. Combine cinnamon with frankincense, myrrh, and sandalwood for a strong protection incense.

 Cloves: For protection, exorcism, and good luck. Use cloves to stop gossip and keep other people's negativity from affecting you.

 Hibiscus: For love and psychic enhancement, and as an aphrodisiac. Use hibiscus in a tea before divination and to encourage psychic dreams. Add it to wine to enhance passion.

 Lemongrass: For inspiring lust and enhancing psychic power. Use in an infusion to promote psychic abilities. Use it in potions for romantic encounters. Planted around your garden, it will discourage the presence of snakes.

Lettuce: For protection, love, divination, and sleep. Grow it to protect your property. Include it in meals to enhance the desire for chastity and fidelity.

Lilac: For exorcism and protection. Planted in your garden, lilacs are believed to keep evil at bay. Place bouquets of lilacs to clear a dwelling of unwanted spirits.

Mugwort: For divination and spirit contact. Drink as a tea before a divination session. Burn it to enhance spirit contact and strengthen your mediumship abilities.

Nutmeg: For luck, money, and health. Carry it in your wallet to bring prosperity, ensuring that you'll always have cash. Add it to a tea to enhance psychic visions.

Patchouli: For money, fertility, and lust. Burn patchouli to bring prosperity, especially in a place of business. Carry patchouli to bring money to you.

Peppermint: For purification, psychic powers, healing, and sleep. Burn as an incense to bring good health during the winter. Drink it as a tea before bed to bring prophetic dreams.

Sage: For healing, protection, and cleansing. Use sage smoke to cleanse your living space from unwanted energy and entities.

Star anise: For protection, purification, psychic powers, and luck. Place small bags of star anise around your home for protection and consecration. Burn it as incense for meditation in powdered form.

Thyme: For health, healing, and visions. Wear it when using a divination tool. Use the dried herb in spells for good health or healing.

Valerian: For dreams, sleep, and protection. Valerian is a substitute for cemetery dirt. Burn to clear and cleanse a ritual space. Use for dream magic and in baths to enhance protection.

Vanilla: For love, seduction, and mental powers when clarity and concentration are required. Use in love sachets and mojo bags. Wear the oil to enhance your powers of seduction.

BALMS, SALVES, AND OILS

The most common use for oils, salves, and magical balms is to anoint an object for a particular intention. Using them in anointing candles and within candle magic serve as a perfect example. You can also anoint yourself before a ritual or spell crafting, but make sure that the ointment you use is safe for your skin. The green witch embraces her magic potions, but safety is always first.

In this section, all the herbs used in the following recipes will be *dried* herbs. Choose your base oil or balm material thoughtfully and considering what works best for you in your practice. Your chosen bases can be expensive carrier oils but they need not be costly. Grapeseed oil is divine but a less expensive olive oil will work wonders; the more economical vegetable oil will make your magic no less potent.

BREATHE EASY ROSEMARY BALM

The power of rosemary has long been used for purification and the clearing of negative energy, to aid in sleep, and for protection. Rosemary promotes healing, so it's often used in poppets (dollies made for magical use) and would be perfect for anointing a healing candle. Used on candles for love spells, this rosemary balm will manifest and amplify honorable intentions. Applied to your chest, it will help clear congestion from a cold.

TOOLS YOU WILL NEED:

- ✶ Balm base: petroleum jelly, 3 or 4 tablespoons for a small jar
- ✶ Small saucepan
- ✶ Herbs: rosemary
- ✶ Small jar with lid
- ✶ Essential oil: eucalyptus

TO MAKE THE BALM:

In a small saucepan, melt the petroleum jelly on the stovetop over low heat. Add the rosemary and stir. Pour the mixture into a jar and add several drops of eucalyptus oil to it for the strength you desire. Cap the jar and allow it to cool and thicken before use.

BLESSING OIL

Blessing oil can be used to anoint an amulet or a special piece of jewelry. On your altar, use it to anoint your ritual tools or special altar items. It can also be applied to your body before spell crafting, or divination, to help you reach a higher vibrational level. This oil may also be used before rituals to anoint candles or people for handfastings, wiccanings, sabbat, or esbat celebrations. Blessing oil carries in it the element of Spirit, no matter what your personal path may be.

TOOLS YOU WILL NEED:

- ⁕ A glass jar
- ⁕ Essential oil: lavender
- ⁕ Stones: 1 small rose quartz
- ⁕ Herbs: 3 parts lavender (approximately 3 pinches or 3 teaspoons), 2 parts sage (approximately 2 pinches or 2 teaspoons), and 1 part myrrh (approximately 1 pinch or 1 teaspoon)

TO MAKE THE OIL:

In a glass jar, combine the essential oil, rose quartz stone, and herbs. Allow this to steep in the sun for one day and the moonlight for one night. This oil can be used as an all-purpose blessing oil, to be used on yourself or on any number of magical items and tools.

ROSE PETAL SALVE

Rose petal salve can be used to anoint candles to attract love, applied to the heart chakra to help soothe the grief and pain of heartache, and used to anoint items belonging to a couple to end strife and bring peace. This salve is excellent for magical spells pertaining to beauty, as roses are the epitome of physical attractiveness and charm.

TOOLS YOU WILL NEED:

- ⚹ A jar with a lid
- ⚹ Stones: 1 small rhodochrosite
- ⚹ A small saucepan
- ⚹ Base: petroleum jelly, 3 or 4 tablespoons for a small jar
- ⚹ Spoon
- ⚹ Herbs: 3 parts rose petals or 3 pinches (approximately 3 teaspoons)
- ⚹ Essential oil: rose

TO MAKE THE SALVE:

In the bottom of the empty jar, place the rhodochrosite. In a small saucepan, melt the petroleum jelly over low heat; stir to make sure it melts evenly. Once the petroleum jelly has melted, add the rose petals and essential oil. Pour the mixture into the jar. After it has cooled slightly, cap the lid. Allow it to cool completely and thicken before use; this may take two or three hours.

SOOTHE THE MIND MEDITATION OIL

Lavender and amethyst are united in this oil to calm and center, to bring prophetic dreams and visions, and to enhance your natural psychic ability. This oil is also excellent for stilling your mind during meditation, grounding you, and allowing universal vibrations of clarity and empowerment to flow through you.

TOOLS YOU WILL NEED:

- ⚹ A glass bottle with a lid or cork
- ⚹ Stones: 3 small amethyst
- ⚹ Base oil
- ⚹ Herbs: lavender, mugwort, and chamomile
- ⚹ Essential oil: lavender
- ⚹ Candle: 1 lavender votive (optional)

In the glass bottle, place the amethyst stones, oil, dried herbs, and as many drops of essential oil for the strength you desire. You can place this bottle on an altar, a windowsill, or a small table and burn a lavender votive candle beside it, to which you have imbued the intention of peace, second sight, and an opening of the third eye. Burn the candle to completion and toss any remaining remnants in a green, growing garden area or your nearest trash bin.

BLESSED BE MY HOME BASIL BALM

Basil balm can be applied to your front door, and used to anoint windowsills, as a means of blessing your house with peace and prosperity. It can also be used to anoint a talisman hung on or near the entrances of a home to keep people with negative intentions away. Though adding oregano is optional, including this herb bolsters the energy, discouraging troublesome in-laws from entering your home.

TOOLS YOU WILL NEED:

- A glass jar with a lid
- Base: petroleum jelly, 3 or 4 tablespoons for a small jar
- A small saucepan
- Spoon
- Herbs: basil and oregano (optional)

TO MAKE THE BALM:

In a small saucepan, melt the petroleum jelly over low heat. Add the basil and oregano (if using). Pour the mixture into the jar and cap it. Allow it to cool and thicken before use.

MARS ASTROLOGICAL OIL

Mars astrological oil promotes courage, bravery, strength, aggression, and sexual energy. It is an excellent oil to use in defensive magic or to promote healing after surgery. The preparation of this oil can be strengthened many times over by working in close alignment with the astrological energies. I suggest preparing this oil on a waxing moon but you can go even more into alignment. For example, I prepare this oil on Tuesday, the day associated

continued →

with Mars, and use an astrological chart to find the particular hour of a Tuesday that corresponds with Mars. For my geographic location that is either the first hour after sunrise or the third hour after sunset, but you should work from wherever you are and time it to your setting.

TOOLS YOU WILL NEED:

* Base oil: grapeseed oil, olive oil, or vegetable oil
* Herbs: 3 parts allspice (3 pinches or approximately 3 teaspoons), 2 parts cumin (2 pinches or approximately 2 teaspoons), 1 pinch ginger (approximately 1 teaspoon), 1 pinch powdered cloves (approximately 1 teaspoon)
* Essential oil: cloves

TO MAKE THE OIL:

Fill the glass bottle with the oil, herbs, and several drops of clove oil for the strength you desire. Leave this bottle to sit for a day to bathe in the sunlight.

BLACK CAT OIL

This oil can be used to anoint spell candles, naming papers, or other objects for spells of love and attraction. It can also be used for protection by anointing candles, or spell papers, or the items used to make poppets or mojo bags, talismans, or amulets. Black cat oil is the number one oil to use before a mediumship or tarot card reading. Be sure not to harm a black cat when collecting a snippet of its fur; think about using a relaxing grooming session to acquire it.

TOOLS YOU WILL NEED:

* Base: almond oil (to draw in love) and castor oil (to draw in spirits)
* Herbs: sage, bay leaves, myrrh (to substitute for myrhh, use anise, cloves, lemon balm, or cinnamon)
* A small saucepan
* Spoon
* Glass bottle with lid
* Iron nail
* Pinch of steel wool
* Black cat hair

TO MAKE THE OIL:

In a small saucepan, combine the oil and herbs over low heat, just until the herbs release their energy and you can smell them. Don't allow this mixture to come to a boil. Pour the warmed oil into a glass bottle. Add the iron nail, a pinch of steel wool, and the black cat hair. Cap the bottle and allow it to cool in a still, dark place.

FIERY WALL OF PROTECTION OIL

This oil is used for the primary purpose of protection and literally to keep someone from bothering you. It creates a barrier between you and anything or anyone in life that you feel you need protection from. You can anoint your front door to keep enemies away; your wrists, shoes, vehicle, or purse for protection; protective talismans or amulets; or candles to be burned during a protection spell.

TOOLS YOU WILL NEED:

- ✳ Mortar and pestle
- ✳ Herbs: powdered dragon's blood (3 pinches or approximately 3 teaspoons) and solid resins of frankincense and myrrh (approximately 1 tablespoon each)
- ✳ Coarse sea salt, at least 2 teaspoons
- ✳ Glass bottle with lid
- ✳ Base: castor oil, enough to fill the bottle you've chosen

TO MAKE THE OIL:

Using the mortar and pestle, take the solid resins of frankincense and myrrh, which are similar to chunks of sap or natural gum, and grind them to a powder. In a bowl, combine the frankincense and myrrh with the powdered dragon's blood and sea salt and mix well. Pour this mixture into a bottle of castor oil and shake it up.

How else might you use balms, salves, and oils in your practice?

_____

_____

_____

ELIXIRS AND TINCTURES

Elixirs refer to curative drinks or liquids with positive properties for mundane or magical purposes (like an elixir of psychic ability). Elixirs may contain 15 to 50 percent alcohol to dissolve the magical or active compound, if desired. Tinctures refer to a plant extract with a high content of alcohol that you can drink **or** with a high content of essential oils to be applied to the skin. The effects may be magical or medicinal.

A crystal elixir can be incredibly easy to make. Basically, you add a crystal to your drinking water, and you've created a crystal elixir. However, not all crystals are safe to add to consumable elixirs, and if you're using crystals that you're not sure of, you can use an "indirect" method of creating a crystal elixir. This simply means that you don't add the crystal directly to your water.

One simple method is to set your sealed thermos or tumbler filled with water in a bowl, and add an inch or two of water and the toxic crystal or stone to that bowl. Let this sit overnight. In the morning, remove your container from the bowl of charged water, and voilà, you have charged your drinking water with the energy of a stone without endangering your health.

Be Careful with Your Crystals

While many crystals and stones are perfectly harmless to work with in your daily magic, here are just a few of the crystals and stones that are toxic. Do not put these crystals in your mouth or use them in any liquid that you ingest. The crystals listed here should only be used to make tinctures with the *indirect* method.

Amazonite contains copper

Angelite will convert to gypsum when immersed in water

Aquamarine contains aluminum

Azurite contains copper

Black tourmaline contains aluminum

Boji stones contain sulfur

Celestite contains strontium

Chrysocolla contains copper

Lapis Lazuli the pyrite inclusions contain sulphur

Malachite is poisonous

Pyrite contains sulphur

CRYSTAL MEDITATION ELIXIRS

CONSUMABLE

Drawing from an array of crystals when crafting your elixirs, you can achieve an expanse of magical effects. You can use the following crystals on their own, or in a combination, for this crystal tincture:

AMETHYST: This elixir will help you curb addictions and spontaneous behavior of over-indulgence. It will help alleviate insomnia and promote a peaceful night's sleep. This stone also reduces stress and strengthens mental faculties for a clearer more focused mind. Amethyst is the stone of the crown chakra, and this elixir is excellent for meditation and connection with the divine.

ROSE QUARTZ: This is a stone of unconditional love and peace. This elixir can be used to draw love to you, as well as promoting self-love. This crystal is an emotional healer that can help us deal with grief and heartache in a gentle and natural way. Rose quartz, and this elixir, are filled with loving vibrations that will enhance your life on many levels.

CLEAR QUARTZ CRYSTAL: This crystal contains every color in the rainbow and is aligned to the vibrational level of each one. The elixir made with this crystal is a deep-soul cleanser that also navigates the energy and realm of karma, clearing and recharging our mind and body and soul. Clear quartz lends itself to healing in both general ways and very specific healing on a personal level. This elixir will also enhance your metaphysical and psychic abilities.

TOOLS YOU WILL NEED:

- ⁎ Stones: amethyst, rose quartz, and clear quartz crystal
- ⁎ A thermos or large tumbler with lid
- ⁎ Water

TO MAKE THE ELIXIR:

Simply place your chosen stone, or stones, in a tumbler or thermos filled with water.

MONEY-DRAWING HERBAL TINCTURE

TOPICAL

Use this money-drawing tincture to anoint stones used for this purpose, particularly stones carried in your wallet or purse. You can also anoint your wallet or purse, and candles for money spells. The most popular method for using this mixture is to sprinkle it on the walkway leading to your front door, whether it's your home or your business. When you do this, you will be drawing money and prosperity to you.

TOOLS YOU WILL NEED:

- ⚹ A glass bottle with a lid or cork
- ⚹ Spring water
- ⚹ Herbs: dried mint, powdered cinnamon, and whole allspice and cloves
- ⚹ Essential oil: cinnamon
- ⚹ A shredded one-dollar bill (optional)
- ⚹ 4 coins: a penny, nickel, dime, and quarter (optional)

Add the ingredients to a bottle of your choosing filled with spring water. This tincture will smell divine, and you'll notice that the older it gets, the better it smells.

SWEET SLEEP HERBAL TINCTURE

CONSUMABLE

Thoughtfully ingesting this tincture may help on those nights when you just can't quiet your mind and get the rest your body so dearly needs.

TOOLS YOU WILL NEED:

- ⚹ Herbs: dried chamomile, lavender, and valerian
- ⚹ A bottle of sweet tea

Add a small pinch of each of the dried herbs to a bottle of sweet tea. Keep refrigerated. At bedtime, take 2 tablespoons of this tincture. If you prefer, pour a small libation of not more than ⅓ cup, and drink this. Enjoy a peaceful night's sleep.

FOUR THIEVES VINEGAR

CONSUMABLE AND TOPICAL

Four thieves' vinegar is often used topically to anoint candles, name papers, and other items in banishing spells, as well as spells to drive away danger, spells to save an individual from disaster, and any number of spells for protection.

As the story goes, there were four thieves during the time of the black plague in Europe who were robbing the dead but not coming down with the disease. Legend has it that they had created a concoction which, when ingested, prevented them from getting sick.

TOOLS YOU WILL NEED:

* Herbs (choose four): black pepper, coriander, lavender, mint, rosemary, sage, thyme, and garlic
* A glass bottle or jar with lid
* Red wine or apple cider vinegar

1. Combine your chosen herbs in the glass jar or bottle with the red wine or apple cider vinegar. Shake it well.

2. Leave this bottle to sit in a dark and secret place for four days. Shake the bottle once a day during this time. After four days, your bottle of four thieves' vinegar is ready to use.

The Sacred Cup

The chalice is a sacred symbol of the feminine, representing the womb, where all life begins. It's also connected to the element of water, and in some pagan paths is used in tandem with the athame (ritual knife) in the reenactment of The Great Rite, the joining of male and female divinity.

Your ritual chalice can be any type of goblet that appeals to you, whether pewter, silver, or ceramic, though you should choose carefully if you plan to drink from it or serve ceremonial wine. You'll also find several beautiful and inspiring chalices at your local new-age shop that are lovely to look at and aligned with your spiritual path through the design and images.

The chalice is used during rituals for esbats and sabbats, often passed around the circle from practitioner to practitioner, sharing a libation and in this way joining their energy with their coven brothers and sisters and chanting, "May you never thirst." The chalice can also be used by the solitary practitioner in the same way. Most often, a small portion of the beverage is left in the bottom of the chalice to be poured upon the ground, shared as a libation for Mother Earth.

What might your ideal chalice or sacred cup look like? Draw it, if you like.

LEAF NOT YOUR POWER: MAGICAL TEAS TO BREW

The green witch knows that there is magic in herbs and in the teas that can be created from these herbs. Creating a cup of tea steeped with specific herbs for a magical intention is called "tea magic," and witches that focus their practice primarily around the creation and drinking of these enchanted teas are called "tea witches."

As popular as this concept seems today, tea's magical uses have been in play since the ancient times. According to legend, tea itself was first discovered by the Chinese Emperor Shennong in 2737 BCE, and this discovery was quite accidental: Leaves of tea fell into a cup of hot water and the ensuing aroma was enough encouragement to taste it.

The green witch has long been connected with the practice of crafting herbal teas, from the legends of the proverbial old woman and her herbal concoctions to the modern urban witch incorporating the ancient custom of magical teas.

The magical tea recipes listed here will contain actual tea as a base. You can use loose teas for this purpose and steep them in a lovely teapot, a relaxing ritual to do in itself, or you can use tea bags and hot water from a kettle. The choice, and preference, is entirely unique to each green witch, but these teas and their correspondences will help guide your own tea magic.

Black Tea: Black tea has a high caffeine content, and it's this tea that is most commonly used in many bought brands of tea bags. Black tea is created by fermenting the leaves of Camellia sinensis and has a stronger flavor than other varieties.

Magical properties of black tea: banishing, money and prosperity spells, stimulation of the mind (creativity), courage, and self-confidence

Correspondences:

Energy: masculine

Planet: Mars

Element: fire

Season: winter

Crystal: obsidian

Color: black and red

White Tea: White tea is created from the very young, or minimally processed leaves, of the Camellia sinensis plant. When this tea is brewed, it's pale yellow in color.

Magical properties of white tea: cleansing, aura healing, protection, spirit contact, beauty, new beginnings, and psychic abilities

Correspondences:

Energy: masculine

Planet: Mars and sun

Element: air and fire

Season: spring

Crystal: quartz

Color: white, yellow and golden

Green Tea: Green tea is also made from Camellia sinensis but has not undergone the fermenting process used to create black tea. It has a much smoother flavor. This tea is traditionally used in Chinese and Indian medicine for a variety of purposes and is highly noted for its curative qualities.

Magical properties of green tea: health, love and passion, money, banishing negativity

Correspondences:

Energy: masculine

Planet: Mars

Element: fire

Season: summer

Crystal: malachite

Color: orange and green

The herbs listed in each recipe are to be added to your tea to taste. Usually a pinch will do. It's also generally noted if the herbal ingredients are powdered or whole, *they will always be dried, not fresh.* The teas required are all listed in tea bag form, but if you want to modify this and steep loose tea in your teapot, by all means, do that.

MEDITATIVE TEA

TOOLS YOU WILL NEED:

* Herbs: fennel, anise, and a pinch of powdered cinnamon
* Tea: black tea bag

* A cup
* Teakettle
* Hot water

Meditation is almost synonymous with the idea of a stilled mind. Yet, the result of mediation should be new ideas and perspectives, new connections with Spirit and with our own consciousness. In order to be able to achieve this from our private meditation, we need to stimulate the mind so that it is active and curious but not distracted. That's what this meditation tea should do for you.

CALMING TEA

TOOLS YOU WILL NEED:

* Herbs: chamomile and lavender
* Tea: white tea bag
* A cup

* Teakettle
* Hot water
* Music (optional)

To find peace and calm jittery nerves from a busy, hectic day, sit back with this calming tea and listen to some quiet reflective music, the kind with the soothing sound of water running in the background. Sometimes daily life throws an awful lot at us, and we just need to sit back and chill. You can do that while you sip a cup of this tea.

EMPOWERMENT TEA

TOOLS YOU WILL NEED:

- ☆ Herbs: whole allspice, whole cloves, and celery seed
- ☆ Tea: black tea bag
- ☆ A cup
- ☆ Teakettle
- ☆ Hot water

Sometimes we realize when coming through life and experiencing all its connections to other people and a variety of circumstances that our egos may have taken a slight bruising. We may begin to doubt our ability to accomplish something or to make a needed decision. We may need to regenerate our faith in ourselves and our ability to find the needed strength to get on with life. This tea may not solve all your problems, but it will give you a sense of renewed energy and self-confidence to step up to life's plate and carry on.

DIVINATION TEA

TOOLS YOU WILL NEED:

- ☆ Herbs: mugwort
- ☆ Tea: white tea bag
- ☆ A cup
- ☆ Teakettle
- ☆ Hot water

This delicious cup of tea will open the door to your psychic abilities. It will flood your energy with open, loving vibrations that will connect easily with the spirit world. Mugwort has long been used before divination practices to relax our inhibitions and release our intuition, paving the way for meaningful spirit communication. It's not that this ability doesn't come naturally to us, but it's that the modern world and stress we experience may put obstacles in the way. This divination tea will help to remove those obstacles.

DRAWING LOVING VIBES TEA

TOOLS YOU WILL NEED:

- Herbs: rose hips, mint, and a pinch of powdered cardamom
- Tea: green tea bag

- A cup
- Teakettle
- Hot water

This tea may be steeped to draw all kinds of love, including energy and vibrations from angels or spirit guides. It's also excellent when there is the need to reconnect with self-love. When the world seems a bit harsh, and your day has been filled with negative energy or emotions, drinking a cup of this tea will help realign you (and your heart chakra) with the loving energy needed for health and peace. Once the door to loving vibrations has been opened, you may be pleasantly surprised at what crosses the threshold.

PROTECTION TEA

TOOLS YOU WILL NEED:

- Herbs: powdered ginseng, whole cloves, rosemary
- Tea: white tea bag

- A cup
- Teakettle
- Hot water

Protection tea is a good tea to drink at least once a month, whether you think you feel the need or not. It's like clearing the air and space around you, as well as your spirit, from anything or anyone that might complicate your life or cause harm in some way. This doesn't have to be something big, scary, and dangerous. There are little things in life that we need protection from, little things that tarnish the energy around us in such subtle ways that we may not be immediately aware of it. Protection tea will take care of those little things.

ELEMENTAL TEAS

The following teas will align with the energies of the elements: earth, air, fire, and water. Each of these elements influences our lives in some way, or inspires us on some level, and the following teas will enhance this connection between you and each of the four elements.

The type of tea that you use as a base for these elemental recipes, whether black or white or green, will be entirely your own choosing. And again, though these recipes call for a tea bag and a teakettle of hot water, should you wish to use loose tea and steep it in your favorite teapot, that's up to you.

EARTH TEA

The element of earth and this tea will ground you, preparing you for ritual, spell crafting, meditation, or healing. It will reconnect you with the physical world and manifestation in this realm. This tea will amplify and sharpen the physical aspect of the world around you, bringing a renewed connection to nature.

TOOLS YOU WILL NEED:

- Herbs: peppermint, a pinch of powdered thyme, and a few blackberries (fresh or frozen)
- Tea: black, white, or green tea bag
- A cup
- Teakettle
- Hot water

Add the bag of tea you've chosen, along with the herbs, to your teapot or cup and allow to steep for 5 to 15 minutes. Drink this tea and feel physically connected to the earth and the energy around you. You'll feel grounded and focused, ready for magical connections.

AIR TEA

The tea for air will open you and your throat chakra for free-flowing communication. The element of air will inspire and expand your creative juices, reconnecting you to your muse. This tea will sharpen your mental faculties, setting the tone for new learning experiences.

TOOLS YOU WILL NEED:

- Herbs: anise and marjoram
- Tea: black, white, or green tea bag
- A lemon slice
- A cup
- Teakettle
- Hot water

Add the bag of tea you've chosen, along with the herbs and lemon, to your teapot or cup and allow to seep for 5 to 15 minutes. You'll feel inspired for creativity and open to clear, eloquent communication.

FIRE TEA

The element of fire and this tea will ignite you with passion, both physical and mental passion. Fire will propel you to take action, energizing you for physical activities, imbuing you with courage, gusto, and a small measure of bravado.

TOOLS YOU WILL NEED:

- Herbs: cinnamon, ginger, and fennel
- Tea: black, white, or green tea bag
- A cup
- Teakettle
- Hot water

Add the bag of tea you've chosen, along with the herbs, to your teapot or cup and allow to seep for 5 to 15 minutes. You'll feel a renewed sense of passion and purpose and an increased energy level, both physically and mentally.

WATER TEA

The element of water keeps you in touch with your emotions and your intuition. Drink this tea before bed for prophetic dreams and before practicing divination. This tea may also be served to both you and a potential romantic interest. If the recipient is open to your charms, this tea will make that very evident. If not, no harm is done.

TOOLS YOU WILL NEED:

- ✴ Herbs: hibiscus, cardamom, and fennel
- ✴ Tea: black, white, or green tea bag
- ✴ A cup
- ✴ Teakettle
- ✴ Hot water

Add the bag of tea you've chosen, along with the herbs, to your teapot or cup and allow to seep for 5 to 15 minutes. Your psychic abilities will be strong and sensitive, you'll find yourself feeling very open to emotions of love, and you'll find your dreams very vivid and often prophetic.

BELTANE TEA

Beltane is the season to express your physical love and desire for your partner. It's a time to wallow in the wondrous delight of an adult relationship with all the passion and gusto you can spark. To many, this festival and its energy is an absolute celebration of life and the continuation of our existence on a physical level. Share a cup of this tea with your love, whether on a Beltane night or not, and reaffirm your magical connection.

TOOLS YOU WILL NEED:

- ✴ Herbs: hibiscus, cinnamon, and cardamom
- ✴ Tea: green tea bag
- ✴ A cup
- ✴ Teakettle
- ✴ Hot water

Add the bag of tea you've chosen, along with the herbs, to your teapot or cup and allow to seep for 5 to 15 minutes. Sharing a cup of Beltane tea with your partner will expand and magnify the passion of your physical connection. Sharing a cup of this tea with friends for a Beltane celebration will intensify the feeling of camaraderie and celebration. Either way, enjoy!

LUCID DREAMS TEA

Some people have the ability to lucid dream at will, and then there are those of us who need a bit of help. Lucid dreaming is the ability to maintain conscious awareness while dreaming and to be aware of your ability to control the dream. Often, much can be learned and this tea will help you get there.

TOOLS YOU WILL NEED:

- ✶ Herbs: anise, mugwort, and cinnamon
- ✶ Tea: white tea bag
- ✶ A cup
- ✶ Teakettle
- ✶ Hot water

Add the bag of tea you've chosen, along with the herbs, to your teapot or cup and allow to seep for 5 to 15 minutes. By drinking this tea, you've paved the way for a night of incredible and often intense dreams.

FERTILITY TEA

Whether you desire fertility of mind, body, or spirit, this tea will put you on the path to your goal. Preferably drink this tea before bedtime, so that while you sleep, the magic works. While we sleep, our subconscious mind is more open to possibilities that the universe might be sending us. This tea will open the door and let in the light. Of course, complement this with visits to your doctor, specialist, or chosen healthcare provider as well.

TOOLS YOU WILL NEED:

- ✶ Herbs: ginseng, peppermint, and allspice
- ✶ Tea: green tea bag
- ✶ A cup
- ✶ Teakettle
- ✶ Hot water

Add the bag of tea you've chosen, along with the herbs, to your teapot or cup and let steep for 5 to 15 minutes. Absorb the energy and magic of infinite possibilities and a renewed sense of purpose, laced with the energy of success.

TEA NOTES AND REFLECTIONS

_____

_____

_____

_____

_____

_____

_____

_____

_____

_____

_____

_____

_____

_____

_____

_____

OF SACRED CAKES AND BLESSED BREAD: MAGICAL RECIPES TO EAT AND OFFER

Just as other spiritual practitioners have used bread and wine as part of their ritual for centuries, so pagan practitioners have long incorporated food and drink as a way of connecting with divinity, honoring a full moon or sabbat, or connecting with Spirit through solitary rituals.

The Green Witch's Kitchen Tips

By embracing these simple tips, you'll make the most of your magical kitchen.

Cleared Space: Keep a pot of growing sage to keep the energy in this area positive and cleared of undesirable energies.

Enhancing Psychism: Foods meant to ignite psychic abilities are best prepared on a waxing or full moon, and on Monday (moon).

Inspiring Lust and Love: Foods to inspire lust and love are best prepared on a Friday (Venus) and during a waxing moon.

Kitchen Tools: Your kitchen tools translate into magical tools. Spoons become magic wands. Your kettle becomes your cauldron. Your oven is a magical hearth. Your carving knife becomes your athame. Every tool that you use in your kitchen carries the potential for sacred use, and every tool in your kitchen used for the preparation of ceremonial foods can be cleansed and consecrated before this process begins.

Magical Cookbook: Keep a special notebook for magical and ceremonial recipes.

Moon Phase: Prepare foods to manifest something to you on the waxing moon, and foods that are meant to banish or exorcise on the waning moon.

Sacred Utensils: Consider using a separate set of utensils and pans reserved solely for preparing your magical recipes.

Set Intentions: When crafting a recipe stay focused, on task, and create with your intention in mind.

Sigils and Symbols: When baking pies, inscribe the crust with sigils and symbols on the top crust, or on the bottom crust, so that it's secret.

Stirring Smart: For positive intentions when manifesting recipes, stir *deosil* (clockwise) to banish; for recipes meant to undo something, stir *widdershins* (counterclockwise).

The Green Witch's Herbs

Turn to these herbs to help accomplish a variety of magical goals within your sacred recipes and preparations.

Allspice: money, luck, and healing

Anise: protection, purification, and youth

Basil: love, exorcism, wealth, and protection

Bay: protection, psychic powers, healing, purification, and strength

Cardamom: lust and love

Cinnamon: spirituality, success, healing, power, psychic powers, lust, protection, and love

Cloves: protection, exorcism, love, and money

Coriander: love, health, and healing

Cumin: protection, fidelity, exorcism, and protection against theft

Dill: protection, money, lust, and love

Fennel: protection, healing, and purification

Garlic: protection, purification, and exorcism

Ginger: love, money, success, and power

Licorice Root: lust, love, and fidelity

Marjoram: protection, love, health, happiness, and money

Mint: money, good fortune, and prosperity

Oregano: exorcism and protection

Rosemary: protection, love, lust, mental powers, exorcism, purification, healing, sleep, and youth/beauty

Sage: purification, exorcism, protection, and longevity

Thyme: love, purification, courage, health, healing, sleep, and psychic powers

THE GREEN WITCH'S RECIPES

With these recipes, you'll find something for nearly every occasion, letting you bring the magic into your food and drink.

CELEBRATORY CITRUS COOKIES

This is a tasty morsel to serve your guests in honor and celebration of a baby's arrival. Bake this shortbread with the intentions of a blessed and peaceful life, for prosperity and good health, and most of all . . . for happiness. Serve this after the naming ceremony to spread the magic.

MAKES: 24 COOKIES / PREP TIME: 15 MINUTES, PLUS 45 MINUTES TO CHILL / COOK TIME: 14 MINUTES, PLUS 5 MINUTES TO COOL

* 1 white candle, for blessings (optional)
* 1 cup all-purpose or whole-wheat flour
* ¼ teaspoon fine sea salt
* ⅓ cup granulated sugar, divided
* 1½ teaspoons orange extract
* 1 teaspoon grated lemon peel
* ½ cup unsalted butter, softened
* ½ teaspoon pineapple extract
* Cane sugar, for sprinkling

1. Preheat the oven to 325°F. Light a white candle to sit on or near the stove and help bless your work.

2. In a small bowl, using a sieve or sifter, sift together flour and salt until evenly combined. Set aside.

3. In a mortar, combine 1 tablespoon of granulated sugar, orange extract, and lemon peel and grind lightly with the pestle until the mixture is evenly mixed and fragrant. Bless this by making the sign of the pentacle over the top.

4. Place the mixture in a large bowl. Add the remaining sugar and softened butter. Cream together until smooth and the sugar is evenly combined, and then gently fold in the pineapple extract. Add the sifted flour and salt to the butter mixture a little at a time, folding it in until no flour streaks remain, and it forms a dough. Cover the bowl and refrigerate for 30 minutes.

continued →

Celebratory Citrus Cookies *continued*

5. Line a large baking sheet with parchment paper and set aside. Roll the chilled dough out to roughly ½- to ¼-inch thickness. Using a star-shaped cookie cutter or other favorite shape, cut out shortbread cookies and place each onto the prepared baking sheet. Lightly sprinkle the top of each cookie with cane sugar, then place in the freezer for 15 minutes to chill before baking.

6. Bake cookies for 12 to 14 minutes. Before removing, let cookies cool for 5 minutes. If you like, leave them in an airtight container to bathe in the moonlight for one night.

GREET YOUR GODDESS GREENS

This refreshing garden salad makes the experience of Goddess connection unique at the end of all moon rituals, for pagan get-togethers that celebrate the divine feminine, or for rituals connecting to earth energy and grounding.

MAKES: 4 SERVINGS / PREP TIME: 20 MINUTES

- ✶ 2 heads romaine or butter lettuce, chopped
- ✶ ¼ small red onion, thinly sliced
- ✶ ½ cup walnuts, roughly chopped
- ✶ 1 medium green or yellow bell pepper, finely chopped

- ✶ ¼ cup grated Monterey Jack cheese
- ✶ ¼ cup grated cheddar cheese
- ✶ 6 tablespoons raspberry or lemon vinaigrette dressing

1. In a large bowl, place the lettuce.

2. Add the red onion, walnuts, and bell pepper.

3. Sprinkle grated Monterey Jack and cheddar cheese over the top. Lightly mix the salad, then drizzle with vinaigrette dressing before serving.

STRAWBERRY MOONLIGHT CAKE

Serve this light, fruity cake when you want to bring people together who may have had a falling out, to promote closer platonic relationships, or when some general feel-good energy is just what's needed. The blend of strawberry flavor and sweet sugar will smooth tempers and mellow attitudes.

MAKES: 4 TO 6 SERVINGS / PREP TIME: 20 MINUTES /
COOK TIME: 40 MINUTES, PLUS 1 HOUR TO COOL

FOR THE CAKE:

* 1 pink candle (optional)
* 1 cup granulated sugar
* ½ cup unsalted butter
* 2 eggs
* ½ cup whole milk

* 2 teaspoons strawberry extract
* 1½ cups all-purpose flour
* 1¾ teaspoons baking powder
* 1 pint strawberries, halved

FOR THE GLAZE:

* 1 cup powdered sugar, sifted

* 4 to 5 tablespoons whole milk, plus more as needed

TO MAKE THE CAKE:

1. Preheat the oven to 350°F. Light a pink candle to sit on or near the stove. Grease and flour a 9-inch square baking pan, tapping the pan gently to remove excess flour.

2. In a medium bowl, cream together the granulated sugar and butter until evenly mixed. Beat in the eggs, one at a time, until evenly combined, then add milk and strawberry extract, folding gently.

3. In a medium bowl, combine the flour and baking powder, stirring until evenly mixed. Add the dry ingredients to the creamed mixture, mixing until evenly combined and no flour streaks remain. Pour the batter into the prepared pan.

4. Bake for 30 to 40 minutes. Cake is done when it springs back to the touch, and a knife or toothpick inserted in the center comes out clean.

5. Let the cake cool for 1 hour. Once cooled, arrange the sliced strawberries on top.

continued →

Strawberry Moonlight Cake *continued*

TO MAKE THE GLAZE:

In a small bowl, combine the powdered sugar and milk, adding the milk 1 tablespoon at a time. Whisk gently until evenly combined and the glaze thickens slightly. Pour the glaze over the top of the cake and strawberries.

FULL MOON SPICE COOKIES

This spiced cookie recipe is just waiting for a full moon and a gathering of happy pagans to partake in it. Whether you're celebrating with family or friends, or connecting with this energy in a solitary way, cookies are always the right choice. The cinnamon, allspice, and cardamom are sure to spice things up and pave the way for prosperity and good luck.

MAKES: 24 COOKIES / PREP TIME: 25 MINUTES /
COOK TIME: 15 MINUTES, PLUS 30 MINUTES TO COOL

- ⚹ 1¼ cups all-purpose flour
- ⚹ ¼ teaspoon baking soda
- ⚹ ¼ teaspoon fine sea salt
- ⚹ ½ cup unsalted butter, softened
- ⚹ ½ cup granulated sugar, divided
- ⚹ ¾ cup light brown sugar, firmly packed

- ⚹ 1 egg
- ⚹ 1 teaspoon maple extract
- ⚹ 1 teaspoon cinnamon
- ⚹ 1 teaspoon allspice
- ⚹ 1 teaspoon cardamom

1. Preheat the oven to 350°F. Grease a cookie sheet and set aside.

2. In a medium bowl, sift the flour, baking soda, and salt together. Set aside.

3. In a medium bowl, cream the butter with ¼ cup of granulated sugar and the brown sugar until fluffy. Whisk in the egg and add maple extract. Gradually add the sifted dry ingredients to the wet ingredients, a little at a time, folding until well blended and no flour streaks remain.

4. In a small bowl, mix the remaining ¼ cup of granulated sugar, the cinnamon, allspice, and cardamom until evenly combined.

5. Drop the dough by teaspoonfuls onto the prepared cookie sheet, about 3 inches apart. Sprinkle each cookie evenly with the sugar and spice mixture.

6. Bake for 12 to 15 minutes. Remove from the oven and let the cookies cool for 30 minutes before removing them from the pan.

7. If you like, place the cookies in an airtight container and leave them overnight in the moonlight before serving.

BELTANE LUSTY CHOCOLATE PUDDING

Chocolate is the proverbial food for lust, passion, and love, showcasing just one reason why it's such a popular gift. Celebrate the spirit of Beltane with this delightful immersion into the indulgent energy of chocolate and expect magical connections.

MAKES: 4 SERVINGS / PREP TIME: 5 MINUTES, PLUS 1 HOUR TO CHILL / COOK TIME: 10 MINUTES

* ½ cup granulated sugar
* ⅓ cup unsweetened cocoa powder
* 3 tablespoons cornstarch
* 2 cups whole milk
* 2 teaspoons vanilla extract
* 2 tablespoons walnuts, roughly chopped (for good luck)
* 2 tablespoons cashews, roughly chopped (for love)
* 3 tablespoons shredded coconut (for glamour and attraction)

1. In a microwave-safe bowl, combine the sugar, cocoa powder, and cornstarch. Whisk in the milk a little at a time for a smooth mixture.

2. Place the mixture in the microwave and cook for 3 minutes on high. Stir to combine the mixture, then cook at 1 minute intervals, stirring between intervals, for 2 to 4 minutes more, or until the pudding is glossy and thickens slightly.

3. Fold in the vanilla, followed by the walnuts and cashews.

4. Pour into a bowl and top with shredded coconut.

5. Chill for one hour. Serve cold.

OSTARA MAGICAL EGG SALAD

The fertility and abundance personified in this pagan holiday are enjoyed in this classic recipe. Embrace the energy of Ostara and revitalize your aura with the egg in a wondrously delicious form. Hang on to your hat, fertility may manifest on a variety of levels.

MAKES: 6 TO 8 SERVINGS / PREP TIME: 10 MINUTES / COOK TIME: 15 MINUTES

* 1 white votive candle (for the goddess Eastre)
* 8 eggs
* ½ cup mayonnaise
* 1 teaspoon yellow or Dijon mustard
* ¼ cup chopped scallions
* Salt
* Pepper
* ¼ cup bacon bits (optional)

1. Light the white candle and place it near your working area to welcome Eastre into your kitchen.

2. In a small saucepan, place the eggs and cover with cold water. Bring water and eggs to a boil over medium to high heat. Boil for 10 minutes. Remove the eggs from the hot water and let cool. Once cooled, peel and chop the eggs, and then place in a medium bowl.

3. Fold in the mayonnaise, mustard, and scallions. If using, fold in the bacon bits.

4. Serve the salad between a sliced, toasted bread of your choice or atop mixed greens.

SAMHAIN APPLE CIDER

An autumn classic, apple cider coincides with chilly days, sweaters, a crackling fireplace, or a roaring firepit. This delightful hot mug of libation will highlight any Samhain celebration or gathering. Raise a toast to the ancestors and embrace the dark night.

MAKES: 6 CUPS / PREP TIME: 5 MINUTES / COOK TIME: 10 MINUTES

- ✶ 6 cups apple cider
- ✶ 2 cinnamon sticks, plus more for serving
- ✶ 1 teaspoon whole cloves
- ✶ 1 teaspoon whole allspice berries
- ✶ A small tea ball filled with anise seeds
- ✶ 8 herbal tea bags (such as peach, raspberry, or lemon)

1. In a large (preferably stainless-steel) saucepan, pour the apple cider.

2. Add the cinnamon sticks, cloves, allspice berries, tea ball with anise seeds, and herbal tea bags.

3. Place the saucepan over low to medium heat for 5 to 10 minutes, stirring often, until the cider is warmed and fragrant, but not boiling.

4. Remove from the heat. Discard the cinnamon sticks and remove the tea ball and tea bags. Strain the cider to remove the cloves and allspice berries. Serve in large mugs with a fresh cinnamon stick for stirring.

LITHA FAIRY BERRIES

The fairies of midsummer's eve will gather expectantly around the house, enticed not only by the magic of the longest day of the year but by the wild, unleashed energy of joy and passion found in this tantalizing Litha recipe.

MAKES: ABOUT 12 TO 14 LARGE STRAWBERRIES /
PREP TIME: 15 MINUTES, PLUS 5 MINUTES TO COOL

- ⚡ 16 ounces milk chocolate or dark chocolate chips
- ⚡ 2 tablespoons coconut oil
- ⚡ 2 cups powdered sugar
- ⚡ 1 pint fresh strawberries, leaves and stems intact
- ⚡ Toothpicks

1. In a double boiler, combine the chocolate chips and coconut oil, stirring occasionally until the mixture is melted and smooth. Pour the powdered sugar into a medium bowl.

2. Using toothpicks, spear each strawberry firmly. Dip each strawberry into the chocolate mixture. Once each strawberry has been evenly coated, roll each in powdered sugar, shaking off any excess sugar gently. Lay them on a plate or tray to cool.

3. Serve fresh.

KITCHEN NOTES AND REFLECTIONS

Part Two

FROM SIGILS TO THE STARS: STAR MAGIC & SPELLS FOR UNION, PROTECTION & DIVINATION

In this section, we're going to dive into rituals to celebrate life's milestones. You'll find ceremonies to acknowledge connections, both human and divine, as well as ways to release relationships and protect yourself from life's fallout. We're also going to explore the stars and the astrological energy found in them that add magic to our lives and purpose to our rituals, spell casting, and meditations.

CHAPTER 4

Rituals & Rites: Ceremonies for Love & Light

From birth to death and the span between, we all reach personal milestones that we'll want to celebrate with our friends and family and Spirit. From a baby-naming ceremony, often called a "wiccaning," to handfasting and commitment, all the way to the sunset of our existence and a summerland ritual to acknowledge a life well lived. In these pages, you'll find rituals to mark all of life's memorable occasions.

SPELLS TO WELCOME AND UNITE

Get ready for an abundance of joyful energy as we acknowledge love and commitment, as well as our connections with nature and Spirit in the following rituals. The energy of the green witch will reverberate with positivity, pride, and emotion as they follow their path and stop to highlight, bless, and embark on their remarkable journey.

HANDFASTING

Handfasting is a pagan ritual to publicly recognize a couple and celebrate their relationship with family and friends. Unlike a legal marriage, people who are handfasted have the option, every year and a day, of renewing this partnership or not.

The pagan community has adopted the tradition of "jumping the broom" at the conclusion of a handfasting ceremony, symbolizing the couple's transition from single life to a life of domesticity. This tradition originated in the West African nation of Ghana, and it found its way to America during colonial times and the arrival of African nationals during the slave trade.

TOOLS YOU WILL NEED:

- ☆ Flowers: roses, hibiscus, or red and pink geraniums
- ☆ Candle: 1 white pillar
- ☆ Essential oil: rose, jasmine, or gardenia
- ☆ Small stand or table
- ☆ Stones: rose quartz
- ☆ Broom
- ☆ Matches or lighter
- ☆ Incense: rose, Nag Champa, or jasmine
- ☆ Rings (optional)
- ☆ A white cord or long sash, about 4 feet in length

1. Prepare the altar with the flowers. Anoint the candle with an essential oil and place it on a small stand or table near the couple, arranging the rose quartz on this table as well.

2. If there are guests, wait for them to gather around and take their place or be seated. Let the couple make their entrance, if they are not already at the altar.

3. The priestess/officiant will lay a broom flat on the ground, near the altar, and light the candle and incense. Turning to the couple, they will begin:

   "We gather now to witness the handfasting between this couple before their friends and family, and Spirit. That it is acknowledged throughout the universe and within the world of men, that this couple shall walk the same path."

4. Allow the couple to speak to each other, to exchange personally written vows or proclamations of love and devotion.

5. Invite parents, close friends, or coven members of the couple to approach the altar with gifts or blessings; allowing children and stepchildren to do the same, to feel included; allowing special acknowledgments to grandparents or great-grandparents as a long-lived couple, letting them pass this blessing to the handfasting couple. Any way that the handfasting couple would like to include family or friends into the ritual itself will make the experience rich and very touching.

6. Begin the exchange of rings as follows:

   The priestess/officiant, to the first handfaster: "Do you come of your own free will to publicly declare your love and devotion for your partner?"

   First handfaster: "I do."

   The priestess/officiant: "Place this ring upon their finger."

   The priestess/officiant, to the second handfaster: "Do you come of your own free will to publicly declare your love and devotion for your partner?"

   Second handfaster: "I do."

   The priestess/officiant: "Place this ring upon their finger."

7. The priestess/officiant will retrieve the white sash. Holding it in their hands, they will say:

   "As you have publicly declared yourselves to each other in the bonds of love and devotion, so Spirit will recognize and bless that bond with this cord."

continued →

8. The couple will each present one of their wrists, holding them side by side before the priestess/officiant. As the priestess/officiant wraps and loosely ties the couple's wrists together, they will say:

   "This cord represents your life together. It signifies the devotion each has for the other. It carries the promise of responsibility that follows love, with enduring affection and infinite connection. It is the tie that binds committed hearts to passionate souls."

9. The priestess/officiant will now place the broom between the couple and their family and friends viewing the ceremony, laying it flat on the ground. The couple will turn to face family and friends, their wrists still tied together. The priestess/officiant will say:

   "Over the broom and into your new life, leap now with joy and anticipation and love."

10. As the couple lands on the other side of the broom and stands before their guests, the priestess/officiant says:

    "They came here as two, they leave as one. It is done. Blessed be."

COMMITMENT

This ritual gives a couple an opportunity to acknowledge and bless their newfound journey together and can either be a private ceremony between the couple or include family and friends. With this rite comes the promise of a future yet to be and an anticipation of blessings coming down the road.

TOOLS YOU WILL NEED:

- ☆ Flowers: roses and baby's breath
- ☆ Herbs: dried rosemary
- ☆ Candles: votive candles: 2 red, 2 white, and 2 pink
- ☆ Essential oil: rose, rosemary, or sage
- ☆ Fireproof plate
- ☆ Promise rings (optional)
- ☆ 2 wine glasses and a beverage of your choice
- ☆ Romantic or relaxation music (optional)

✳ Incense: rose jasmine, rosemary, or lemon balm

✳ Matches or lighter

1. To begin, clean out the center of the room, making way for a clear space large enough for you and your partner to sit with some candles.

2. Gather your tools about you.

3. For those herbs and flowers in pots, set them around your space in an arrangement that is pretty and appealing to your senses.

4. Anoint your candles with essential oil and arrange them on a fireproof plate, along with some stones and any dried herbs, and the promise rings. Fill the wine glasses with the beverage or libation you chose.

5. Light the candles and incense. If you've chosen to have music, start playing it now.

6. Both of you sit. It's preferable to sit on the floor facing each other.

7. Now is the time to say what you want to say to each other, to declare your love, to commit yourself to this individual exclusively, and to your future together.

8. First partner, take up a promise ring, and as you place it on your beloved's finger repeat the following words:

   "With this ring, I commit to you my love and fidelity. I commit to you my energy and joy to build toward our future together. I stand, not before you, or behind you, but beside you, that we may walk in unison through this life."

9. Second partner, repeat this process and these vows:

   "With this ring, I commit to you my love and fidelity. I commit to you my energy and joy to build toward our future together. I stand, not before you, or behind you, but beside you, that we may walk in unison through this life."

10. Take up your wine glasses, and toast this moment in unison:

    "Sacred are you to me, sacred from this day forward. Blessed be."

LOVE

This ritual will help you rediscover how to love yourself, particularly after experiencing overwhelming or self-confidence-wounding people or circumstances. Love is part of the healing process for almost anything that touches our heart and emotions, and this ritual will set the stage to reawaken it.

TOOLS YOU WILL NEED:

- ⚝ Broom
- ⚝ Sage smudge stick
- ⚝ Herbs: hibiscus, lemon balm, or patchouli
- ⚝ Stones: green agates, lavender jade, or clear quartz
- ⚝ Fireproof plate

- ⚝ Candle: 1 pink pillar
- ⚝ Sharp object to carve on your candle: a straight pin, pen, small knife, etc.
- ⚝ Essential oil: eucalyptus, sage, or rosemary
- ⚝ Matches or lighter
- ⚝ Pen and journal

1. Choose your space for this ritual, somewhere you can be comfortably seated and where you can write, such as the dining room table, a desk, or a place on the floor in a room that will be quiet and private.

2. Cleanse this space. Sweep the floor. Smudge the area.

3. Gather your tools, and using your intuition, arrange the herbs and stones in a pleasing manner on the plate.

4. Sit and take up the candle, carving upon it symbols, words, names, or numbers that are connected to you and to positive influences and energies in your life.

5. Anoint the candle with essential oil and place it in the center of the fireproof plate, among the herbs and stones.

6. Light the candle and incense.

7. This is the time to take your journal and list a) all the positive people in your life, b) positive experiences you've had over the past five years, c) five things that bring you joy, d) five ways you've brought joy to someone else, and e) a list of things that makes you happy.

8. When this is done, and you've had time to sit and contemplate about the things you've listed and to ponder on those feelings of warmth and love, extinguish your candle. And as you do so, say:

"I love myself. I am unique. I am precious. I freely give and receive love from those around me. I embrace the healing loving energy of Spirit. I embrace the joy that living brings to my soul. I love myself. I love myself. I love myself. I am worthy of receiving love. So mote it be."

COMMUNING WITH NATURE

This is a ritual to reconnect you to the four elements and, through them, to nature in all her glorious aspects. In performing this ritual, you will realign yourself with the energies needed for grounding, spell crafting, and manifestation, as well as the healing of mind, body, and spirit. With this rite, you will be anointing yourself and manifesting a magical connection to the elements, and you will be creating a mojo bag to sustain this connection.

TOOLS YOU WILL NEED:

⋆ Broom

⋆ Sage smudge stick

⋆ Herbs: patchouli or mugwort, for earth; anise or eyebright, for air; bay leaf or cinnamon, for fire; and calamus or spearmint, for water

⋆ Stones: adventurine or green moss agate, for earth; yellow calcite or citrine, for air; red jasper or garnet, for fire; and blue-lace agate or turquoise, for water

⋆ Candles: for each of the four elements: green, yellow, red, and blue

⋆ Blessing oil (page 67)

⋆ Cloth bag, large enough to hold a few stones and some herbs

1. Select your location for this ritual. A quiet room where you won't be disturbed and where you'll have enough space to cast a circle and create a ritual space would be perfect. This ritual can be done outside if you have access to a garden area.

2. Cleanse and smudge this space.

continued →

3. Cast your circle.

4. At the north, place the green candle on a plate and sprinkle the stones, dirt, and herbs you chose for earth around it. Light this candle as you say:

   "Hail to the guardians of the North, by the power of earth, I summon, stir, and call ye' forth to witness this rite and guard this circle."

5. At the east, place the yellow candle on a plate and sprinkle the stones, dirt, and herbs you chose for air around it. Light this candle as you say:

   "Hail to the guardians of the East, by the power of air, I summon, stir, and call ye' forth to witness this rite and guard this circle."

6. At the south, place the red candle on a plate and sprinkle the stones, dirt, and herbs you chose for fire around it. Light this candle as you say:

   "Hail to the guardians of the South, by the power of fire, I summon, stir, and call ye' forth to witness this rite and guard this circle."

7. At the west, place the blue candle on a plate and sprinkle the stones, dirt, and herbs you chose for water around it. Light this candle as you say:

   "Hail to the guardians of the West, by the power of water, I summon, stir, and call ye' forth to witness this rite and guard this circle."

8. Sit in the center of this circle.

9. Anoint yourself, making the sign of the pentacle, with the blessing oil, 1) at your forehead, 2) at your left hip, 3) at your right shoulder, 4) at your left shoulder, and 5) at your right hip, saying:

   "By earth, and air, and fire, and water, may their energy run through me. Blessed be."

10. Sit and ground yourself.

11. Take this time for meditation on nature and the elements. Call their energy to you, individually, and feel yourself connect with the natural energy of the earth and nature.

12. When the time you've allotted yourself for this ritual has passed, take up the cloth bag and begin at the north quarter. Extinguish the flame of the green candle, adding the herbs and stones to your bag, saying:

    "I thank you, guardians of the north, for witnessing this rite and protecting this circle. Fare thee well and blessed be."

13. At the east gate: extinguish the flame of the yellow candle, adding the herbs and stones to your bag, saying:

    "I thank you, guardians of the east, for witnessing this rite and protecting this circle. Fare thee well and blessed be."

14. At the south gate: extinguish the flame of the red candle, adding the herbs and stones to your bag, saying:

    "I thank you, guardians of the south, for witnessing this rite and protecting this circle. Fare thee well and blessed be."

15. At the west gate: extinguish the flame of the blue candle, adding the herbs and stones to your bag, saying:

    "I thank you, guardians of the west, for witnessing this rite and protecting this circle. Fare thee well and blessed be."

16. Dismantle your sacred space. Find a nice place to keep this energy-filled mojo bag close to you, such as in a drawer in a nightstand, a bookshelf where you keep special books, or in a small box in the corner of your closet.

NAMING/WICCANING

A naming (or wiccaning) ceremony is very similar to the Christian version of an infant baptism. You will be acknowledging this human being before Spirit, publicly stating their name, and inviting family and friends to lend their blessings for this new family member.

TOOLS YOU WILL NEED:

- Herbs and flowers: lavender, lily of the valley, daisy, and baby's breath
- Vintage photos or personal items connected to the family (optional)
- Matches or lighter
- Candle: 1 white pillar candle
- Stones: rhodochrosite for a girl, blue lace agate for a boy, selenite or clear quartz crystal for gender neutral
- Incense: lavender or rose
- Candles: votive candles for each of the four elements: green, yellow, red, and blue
- Bowl of salt
- Incense, at the east gate
- Bowl of water

1. Choose a space for this ritual that is appropriate for the number of people you wish to invite, whether a whole troupe of family and friends or just a handful of loved ones.

2. Decorate the altar with the flowers and herbs suggested. The altar may also be decorated in very personal and unique ways, such as with vintage photos of great-grandparents, with special toys, with a piece of jewelry, or some other item relating to your family's heritage and ancestral roots. The more personal you make it, the more aligned the energy will be.

3. When everyone is assembled and ready to begin, light the white pillar candle and incense that you've chosen with it, and place the stones around it. Light the incense at the east quarter and the elemental candles at the north, east, south, and west gates.

4. The parent/priestess will begin:

   "We've come together today to welcome this child into the world and into this family. We've come to acknowledge the miracle of this child before Spirit."

5. Parents/priestess with child move to the north gate:

   "By the power of earth and the guardians of this gate, we present to you this child (name). Bless this child with physical health and prosperity."

   The parent/priestess will place a crystal or two of salt on the baby's tongue.

6. Parents/priestess with child move to the east gate:

   "By the power of air and the guardians of this gate, we present to you this child (name). Bless this child with intelligence and creativity."

   The parent/priestess will use their hand to waft the incense smoke toward the child, smudging him/her.

7. Parents/priestess with child move to the south gate:

   "By the power of fire and the guardians of this gate, we present to you this child (name). Bless this child with passion in all they do and with motivation for success."

   The parent/priestess will hold this child at the south gate and make the sign of the pentacle above them. (The red candle will be burning at this gate, symbolically lending its energy.)

8. Parents/priestess with child move to the south gate:

   "By the power of water and the guardians of this gate, we present to you this child (name). Bless this child with intuition, second sight, and prophetic dreams."

   The parent/priestess will dip their hand into the bowl of water at this gate and anoint the child's forehead.

9. Parents/priestess will return to the altar.

10. Family members may be invited to participate at this time by offering a special blessing or by placing a gift on the altar.

11. The parent/priestess will hold their hand above the child for a final blessing, saying:

    "This child (name) has been presented to the guardians of the watchtowers, that they may know and acknowledge them on this path. May Spirit recognize (name) and touch this child with magic. We rejoice in the creation of this new life and in the journey that lies ahead. Blessed be."

CAKES AND WINE

The idea of sharing food and drink as a way to connect with divinity is not new, nor is it associated solely with the mainstream spiritual practices that encompass Judeo-Christianity. In the pagan world, it's referred to as "cakes and wine" or "cakes and ale." The premise is much the same for all spiritual paths: to forge a physical connection with the Divine.

A cakes and wine ritual may be incorporated into any other ritual that you are doing, whether for a handfasting, a sabbat, an esbat, or a commitment ceremony. This added element will enrich any ceremony and will add a special connection with Spirit.

TOOLS YOU WILL NEED:

* Candles: 1 white pillar; 1 green votive, for earth; 1 yellow votive, for air; 1 red votive, for fire; 1 blue votive, for water
* Herbs: basil, whole cloves, or star anise (for the masculine); catnip, Dittany of Crete, or spearmint (for the feminine)
* Stones: citrine, hematite, or tiger's eye (for masculine or projective energy); emerald, jade, or selenite (for feminine or receptive energy)
* Incense: Nag Champa, sandalwood, or frankincense
* Essential oil: rose, myrrh, rosemary, or sandalwood
* Wine, ale, or a non-alcoholic beverage of your choice
* Plate of cake or bread of your choice
* Wine glass, goblet, or ritual goblet
* Athame

1. This ritual can be performed at your altar.

2. Prepare the altar by decorating it with the white pillar candle, herbs, stones, and incense.

3. Set the four votive candles at the four quarters.

4. Light the candles and incense.

5. At the altar, acknowledge the sacredness of the Divine and your desire to connect, saying: "

   As I/we stand at this altar, I/we come to connect with the wisdom and power of Spirit. Father Sky and Mother Earth, may I/we unite with your energy and be blessed by your magic."

6. Fill the goblet with your chosen beverage.

7. Take up the goblet in one hand and athame in the other hand.

8. Slowly lower the blade of your athame into the goblet, saying:

   "As the god finds joy in his connection with the goddess, so shall we find joy in our connection with Spirit."

9. Lift the dagger from the wine and touch the cake or bread you chose with the tip of it, saying:

   "As the god and goddess rejoice in their union, so shall the earth be blessed with fertility and magic. By the power of Spirit, blessed be."

10. All present may share of the cakes and wine, saving a small libation of each to pour out on the ground as a libation to Mother Earth.

What else might you incorporate into your Cakes and Wine ritual?

_____

_____

_____

_____

_____

_____

_____

_____

SPELLS TO PROTECT, RELENT, AND RELEASE

Just as we embrace rituals and ceremonies to celebrate positive energy and people brought into our lives, so we acknowledge people, situations, and energy that we must release, banish, or block from our space. We do this with grace and dignity, with rites and rituals that respectfully bring closure and manifest change.

HANDPARTING

Every year and a day, pagan handfasting is renewable if both people agree to continue this domestic commitment for another year and a day. However, there are couples for whom this is not the case, and a decision is made to end the relationship. This is a ceremony to acknowledge, dignify, and respectfully observe the process of separation. You'll want to select a special spot, whether it's the living room, a private garden spot, or a clearing along a favorite hiking trail. This ceremony may be conducted with friends and family present, though couples who are separating may prefer to keep this ritual a private matter. Wear your wedding rings, as their removal and disposal are an integral part of this ceremony.

TOOLS YOU WILL NEED:

- ✶ Wedding rings
- ✶ Herbs: wormwood, rosemary, vervain, or camphor
- ✶ Stones: black onyx, black tourmaline, apache tears, or jet
- ✶ Incense: elder, mulberry, sandalwood, or sage
- ✶ Candle: 1 black pillar
- ✶ Essential oil: sage or camphor
- ✶ Matches or lighter
- ✶ Jewelry box

1. Set up your altar by adding to it the herbs, stones, and incense in a pleasant arrangement.

2. Anoint the black pillar candle with the essential oil of your choice and place it in the center of your altar. Light the candle and incense.

3. Stand or sit facing each other. Decide who will speak first.

4. Partner #1 says:

    "We come together today to acknowledge to the universe and to Spirit that we choose to walk separate paths in this world."

5. Partner #2 says:

    "We come together today to acknowledge to ourselves (*optional: and to friends and family) that we are no longer bound by love and commitment, but that our souls will go in different directions."

6. Partner #1 removes their ring, saying:

    "With this ring, I release you from any obligation, magical or mundane, and I place my blessing upon your freedom, that you may find happiness and contentment in the future."

7. Partner #1 lays the ring upon the altar.

8. Partner #2 removes their ring, saying:

    "With this ring, I release you from any obligation, magical or mundane, and I place my blessing upon your freedom, that you may find happiness and contentment in the future."

9. Partner #2 lays their ring upon the altar.

10. Partners #1 and #2 say in unison:

    "As we came into this handfasting together, so we exit this state together. We go now to bury the past and make way for the future."

    (*optional: if you have friends and family present, turn as a couple and speak directly to them.)

11. Take the box containing your wedding rings and bury it beneath a tree, whether on personal property, a city park, a quiet country road, or a hiking spot in the woods. There's a tree somewhere waiting for you and your past, and the universe will lead you to it.

RELEASING NEGATIVE ENERGY

We can all usually tell when negative energy is impacting our life on some level, and the green witch knows to cast out this destructive unpleasant energy and the sensations that it brings with it, and usher in healthy energy to revitalize us and enhance our life.

TOOLS YOU WILL NEED:

* Herbs: wheat, mugwort, or patchouli (for physical healing); anise, marjoram, or sage (for mental healing); cinnamon, allspice, or ginger (for motivation and passion); catnip, myrrh, or sandalwood (for emotional healing)
* Stones: jade or adventurine, yellow calcite or citrine, garnet or red jasper, blue lace agate, or turquoise
* Incense: sage or rosemary
* Essential oil: sage or rosemary
* Candles: 1 green votive, for health and healing physically; 1 yellow votive, for health and healing mentally; 1 red votive, for passion and motivation; 1 blue votive, for health and healing of emotions; 1 white pillar
* Matches or lighter

1. Using your intuition, prepare your altar by placing on it the herbs, stones, and incense in a pleasing arrangement.

2. Anoint your candles with essential oil and place them on the altar among the other items. Light the green candle, saying:

   "As I stand before Spirit, stripped of all pretense, I banish negative energy from my physical being. Be gone from me. Disperse to the four corners of the universe. My body be healed of maladies and pain."

3. Light the yellow candle, saying:

   "As I stand before Spirit, stripped of all pretense, I banish negative energy from my mind. Be gone from me. Disperse to the four corners of the universe. My mind be healed and filled with peace and balance."

4. Light the red candle, saying:

   "As I stand before Spirit, stripped of all pretense, may the energy of motivation and the passion for success fill my space and myself. May this positive energy fill the void and raise me to new heights of awareness."

5. Light the blue candle, saying:

   "As I stand before Spirit, stripped of all pretense, I banish negative energy from my emotions. Be gone from me. Disperse to the four corners of the universe. My emotions be healed and filled with love and contentment."

6. Light the white pillar candle, saying:

   "All negative energy be gone, by the light of this white candle I am bathed in positive energy and the blessings of Spirit. So mote it be."

PROTECTION/WARDING OFF EVIL

The green witch can sense when danger is near and protection is necessary. With their arsenal of magical expertise, they know how to conjure boundaries that will protect them and keep them safe from negative people, situations, fallout, energy, and evil. Whether as a novice or an experienced practitioner, the necessity and the power of this ritual will be clear to you when you sense that danger may be near.

TOOLS YOU WILL NEED:

- ✶ Sage smudge stick
- ✶ Herbs: blessed thistle, belladonna, foxglove, cayenne pepper, garlic, cactus, skunk grass, or St. John's wort
- ✶ Sea salt
- ✶ Candles: 4 black votives
- ✶ Essential oil: rosemary, eucalyptus, or peppermint
- ✶ Matches or lighter
- ✶ 4 small ceramic bowls

1. First, smudge your living space, whether this is a house, an apartment, a trailer or RV, or a single room. Give your space a good cleansing before you begin this ritual to ensure there is no nasty energy already lurking.

2. Figuratively throw up walls of protection around your living space by placing at least three of the herbs listed above around the perimeter.

3. Follow this by sprinkling a line of sea salt around the perimeter, making sure it's a solid, unbroken line.

continued →

Protection/Warding Off Evil *continued*

4. Anoint the four black candles with essential oil and set them up in your space, whether on the kitchen table, an altar, the kitchen counter, or a coffee table.

5. Light the first candle, saying:

   "Guardians of the north gate, protect me from physical danger, that those who wish me harm shall not have access to me."

6. Light the second candle, saying: *"Guardians of the east gate, protect me from harmful negative thoughts, that those who wish me ill may be confused and stifled in this endeavor."*

7. Light the third candle, saying:

   "Guardians of the south gate, protect me from the aggression of those who wish me harm, that they may be depleted of this energy and unable to accomplish their endeavor."

8. Light the fourth candle, saying:

   "Guardians of the west gate, protect me from those who wish to hurt my feelings, wound my ego, or cause grave emotional injury; may they be blocked from this endeavor, that their words and actions are inconsequential to my being."

9. Allow the candles to burn down. The ritual is complete, so security and safety are assured.

10. To maintain your boundary, place four small ceramic bowls of sea salt at the four corners of your space.

RELEASING OLD FRIENDS OR LOVERS

There is no energy or influence in life quite like the overpowering permeating energy of an old lover. Some spiritual paths claim that the energy of lovers, once connected and sparked, will remain intact for all eternity. Not so fast, says the green witch. Through the power of her magic and the will of her manifestation, the green witch will reclaim her energy *and* her life.

TOOLS YOU WILL NEED:

- ⁎ Broom
- ⁎ Sage smudge stick
- ⁎ Candles: 1 black votive, 1 red votive, 1 white votive
- ⁎ Essential oil: cedar or cinnamon
- ⁎ Incense: cedar or cinnamon
- ⁎ Fireproof plate
- ⁎ Matches or lighter
- ⁎ A photo of your old lover (optional)
- ⁎ Birthstone, your old lover's
- ⁎ Cloth
- ⁎ Hammer

1. Prepare an altar area that will provide privacy and space for your candles and a bit of ritual activity. This can be your living room floor, bedroom, the dining room table, a secluded outdoor area in a park, the wilderness, or your own backyard.

2. Cleanse the area by sweeping and smudging. Gather your tools and prepare a space to set up the candles, herbs, and incense.

3. Dress the candles with an essential oil and set them on your altar on a fireproof plate. Light the incense.

4. Stand or sit and begin.

5. Light the red candle, saying:

   "As the energy of this image is released with this flame, so I release the energy of this person from my aura, from my thoughts, and from my space."

6. Light a match, and holding the photo over the fireproof plate, light it ablaze. Drop it onto the fireproof plate and allow it to burn to ash.

7. Light the black candle. Anoint the birthstone with essential oil and wrap it completely in the cloth. Laying it on the floor, or the ground, tap it with the hammer, breaking the stone in the process, saying:

continued →

Releasing Old Friends or Lovers *continued*

"As this stone is shattered, so is this individual's hold on my heart, my emotions, and my life is broken and I am free of their energy, their will, and their influence . . .
So mote it be."

8. Light the white candle and allow all the candles to burn down.

9. Gather up the remnants of this spell and toss it all in the trash can.

SUMMERLAND RITUAL

Death is another of life's milestones, and it's a milestone that needs to be acknowledged and celebrated, just as all other milestones. A summerland ritual is basically a pagan funeral, and it's not really any different than any other funeral: being a celebration of someone's life, a declaration of the love still felt by friends and family, and a send-off to the other side.

TOOLS YOU WILL NEED:

⚹ Herbs: roses, carnations, lilies, and other flowers or herbs that were a favorite of the deceased

⚹ Candles: 4 white pillars

⚹ Essential oil: rose or sage

⚹ Incense: Nag Champa, rose, or a personal favorite

⚹ Matches or lighter

⚹ Personal items belonging to the deceased: old photos, toys, mementos from life, and jewelry (optional)

1. Depending on the venue for this celebration, whether in a private home, in a cemetery, or in a building, set up an altar near the coffin, if the deceased is going to be present. If the deceased will not be present, set up the altar as the center and focus for this ritual.

2. Arrange the flowers and personal mementos in a pleasing arrangement.

3. Anoint the four white pillar candles and place them on the altar with the incense.

4. When all those who will be attending are present, light the incense.

5. The priest/priestess, or a designated family member, will light the first pillar candle, saying:

   "We bless you (name), by the power of earth. We acknowledge and honor the physical body that was you. We recall with love and warmth the comfort that you were, the security your physical presence gave us, and the joy we felt at the sight of you."

6. The priest/priestess, or a designated family member, will light the second pillar candle, saying:

   "We bless you (name), by the power of air. We acknowledge and honor the mental aspect of you. We recall with fondness and warmth the loving thoughts shared, the knowledge passed on, and the humor and wit that were a part of you."

7. The priest/priestess, or a designated family member, will light the third pillar candle, saying:

   "We bless you (name), by the power of fire. We acknowledge and honor the passion and fire of your soul. We recall with admiration and awe your passion for life, your passion for the people you loved and the things that mattered to you. We celebrate this energy now, and we feel its presence."

8. The priest/priestess, or a designated family member, will light the fourth pillar candle, saying:

   "We bless you (name), by the power of water. We recall with wistful longing the human emotions of love, desire, concern, and care that you so freely shared. We celebrate this energy today, as we send you forth on the next level of life's adventure."

9. The priest/priestess, or designated family member, will now come forward to give the eulogy. Then, invite those who wish to share a story or a thought about their loved one to come forward and do so.

10. In closing the summerland ritual, the priest/priestess or designated family member will say:

    "By the power of the elements, earth, air, fire, and water, by the blessing of Spirit, may (name) journey to the summerland be one more wondrous adventure and experience for the soul. Merry we meet; merry we part. Till we merry meet again. Blessed be."

NOTES AND REFLECTIONS

NOTES AND REFLECTIONS

_____

_____

_____

_____

_____

_____

_____

_____

_____

_____

_____

_____

_____

_____

_____

CHAPTER 5

Look to the Stars: Astrological Signs & Celestial Spells

Within this chapter, we're going to delve into the energy of the zodiac signs and the magic found in the stars, sun, and moon for spell crafting, manifestation, and rituals. Though the green witch draws much energy and inspiration from the earth and the plants and herbs grown there, the magical connection would not be complete without including celestial energy within the spiritual practice.

ASTROLOGICAL ZODIAC SIGNS

We're going to connect with the magic of the astrological sun signs in order to harness this impressive energy for spell crafting and manifestation. Just as the green witch embraces the earth and the magical energies found there, they also embrace the stars and claim the celestial power found in the heavens.

Aries

Element: fire

Energy: masculine/projective

Color: red

Physical influences: the head

Celestial influences: beginnings and action

The fiery impulsive energy of Aries lends itself well for spells of strength, power, control, lust, and sex. Aries is the most blatantly passionate sign in the zodiac, with that passion encompassing a wide range of emotions and aspects.

Taurus

Element: earth

Energy: feminine/receptive

Color: pink, pale blue, and green

Physical influences: throat and cerebellum

Celestial influences: manifestation and security

The strong and stubborn energy of Taurus works for spells regarding money and relationships. The obstinate and often blunt demeanor of this sign conceals the actual need for love and affection, as well as material comfort that resides below the surface.

Gemini

Element: air

Energy: masculine/projective

Color: yellow

Physical influences: nervous system, hands, shoulders, arms, and lungs

Celestial influences: movement and mental energy

Gemini's intellectual influence highlights spells for creativity (on a variety of levels), travel, and diplomacy. Be cautious with the energy of Gemini, as its duality can often cause an unexpected shift in spell casting and manifestation, leading to surprising results.

Cancer

Element: water

Energy: feminine/receptive

Color: blue and gray

Physical influences: breast, stomach, and solar plexus

Celestial influences: emotions and home environment

The nurturing, gentle nature of Cancer will beautifully advance the energy for spells of fertility, domesticity, as well as family life and relationships dealing with the issues that arise here. Cancer energy is deeply connected with emotions and the act of getting in touch with those emotions on a base level.

Leo

Element: fire

Energy: masculine/projective

Color: yellow and orange

Physical influences: heart and spine

Celestial influences: success and courage

Leo's energy will spark motivation and ambition, manifesting new opportunities in work or career advancement. This is the energy you will want to use with any magical endeavor geared to inspire courage, leadership, and strength of will.

Virgo

Element: earth

Energy: feminine/receptive

Color: green and brown

Physical influences: intestinal tract

Celestial influences: analysis and service

Virgo's energy and focus lends itself to spells of education, health, and healing. Virgo's connection with Mercury means that the expansion and eloquence of communication are highlighted, as well as an uncanny ability to multitask. If there's confusion around, Virgo's energy can straighten it out.

Libra

Element: air

Energy: masculine/projective

Color: pink, pale green, and blue

Physical influences: kidneys

Celestial influences: beauty and socialization

Libra is all about balance and justice. This is the perfect energy to call up for spells dealing with legal issues. Libra is also all about love and romance, and partnerships above all. The romantic energy of Libra was made to produce manifestation along these lines.

Scorpio

Element: water

Energy: feminine/receptive

Color: red and maroon

Physical influences: generative system and rectum

Celestial influences: regeneration and justice

The darkest and most mysterious sign of the zodiac, Scorpio's energy will inspire spell crafting for divination, healing of addictions, and self-analysis. The elusiveness of this energy may also ironically be used to reveal secrets, as secrets are a highlight of the mysterious Scorpio.

Sagittarius

Element: fire

Energy: masculine/projective

Color: purple and dark blue

Physical influences: hips, thighs, and arterial blood

Celestial influences: idealization and study

Sagittarius is the most independent of the zodiac signs; its energy volatile and outspoken and opinionated. There is great depth of intellectualism to this sign as well, and the energy raised with Sagittarius can be focused on education and new intellectual endeavors.

Capricorn

Element: earth

Energy: feminine/receptive

Color: dark green, gray, black, and brown

Physical influences: knees and skeleton

Celestial influences: building and business

Capricorn is another zodiac sign that is strong and stubborn, set in its ways, and prone to be difficult to manage at times. This energy is also powerful in the capacity for organization, endurance, and determination. Sometimes the stubbornness of Capricorn is exactly what's needed for manifestation.

Aquarius

Element: air

Energy: masculine

Color: blue and turquoise

Physical influences: ankles and circulation

Celestial influences: humanitarian and group energy

Aquarius energy is aloof and often comes across as distant but this sign may be what's needed for spells of self-improvement, spells to enhance self-control, and spells that need a cold steely arms-length look at a situation. Aquarius energy lends itself well to solitary inner workings.

Pisces

Element: water

Energy: feminine/receptive

Color: sea green

Physical influences: feet

Celestial influences: spirituality and transformation

Pisces is the key sign for psychism and spells and meditations for intuition, clairvoyance, lucid dreaming, telepathy, and spirit contact. It's the energy of Pisces that will lend itself to work involving the expansion of spirituality and spiritual awakenings.

ASTROLOGICAL NOTES AND REFLECTIONS

_____

_____

_____

_____

_____

_____

_____

_____

_____

_____

_____

_____

_____

_____

_____

ASTROLOGICAL NOTES AND REFLECTIONS

_____

_____

_____

_____

_____

_____

_____

_____

_____

_____

_____

_____

_____

_____

_____

_____

CELESTIAL SPELLS

The magic and power of the green witch, though entrenched and so closely connected with earth and the world of herbs, will be inspired, uplifted, and enhanced by the inherent magical energy found in the sun, moon, and stars. It's all connected, as the old saying goes. The earth and all its flourishing flora would not exist if not for the miracle of the firmament. This energy, this power found here, is a birthright for all magical practitioners, including the green witch.

DRAWING DOWN THE STARLIT POWER SPELL

We're going to be working with the power of the full moon. How many of us have stood in awe, bathed in the silver light of the moon, transfixed by the feeling of it upon our skin? Whether as a child or an adult, you could feel it as a very real and tangible physical sensation. There is power in this celestial body and in this energy, and we're going to perform a simple ritual to draw this magical energy into ourselves.

TOOLS YOU WILL NEED:

* Incense: any scent of your choice
* Matches or lighter
* A cloak (optional)

* An outdoor location, preferably private or semiprivate and in full view of the moon, such as a city park, a favorite hiking trail, or your own backyard

1. You may choose to perform this ritual skyclad (nude) if you are so lucky as to have a *completely private* yard, field, or land; you might want to have a cloak handy for the before and after ritual moments. If you do not have access to such privacy, you will still benefit from this ritual when fully clothed.

2. From the spot you have chosen, light your incense and stand facing the moon, taking a few moments to still your mind and center yourself.

3. Stand with your feet slightly apart, raise your hands skyward, palms toward the moon, saying:

   "I come before Spirit to be baptized in the sacred light. Bless my feet that have led me to this path. Bless my knees that bend to the ebb and flow of life. Bless my breast that nurtures love, honor, and commitment. Bless my lips that speak the truth. I am blessed before Spirit and willingly embrace the energy of this moon."

4. Lower your arms and take three deep breaths, inhale to the count of three, and exhale to the count of six.

5. Raise your arms once more, palms toward the moon, saying:

   "I stand before you now, Father Sky and Mother Moon. Upon this night, amidst this light, I draw within myself the power and magic of the moon, and the blessings of this celestial energy. Upon this night, amidst this light, I draw within myself the power and magic of the ancestors who stood in this ritual before me. So mote it be."

6. Stay still in this position as long as you feel the desire to do so, or until you stop feeling any physical sensations that often accompany this ritual, such as tingling on the bottoms of your feet or the back of your head.

7. When you feel the moment is right, put your hands down and again take three deep breaths, inhaling to the count of three, and exhaling to the count of six.

SHINE BRIGHTLY AS THE SUNLIT POWER SPELL

This is a spell using the regenerative healing properties of the sun to maintain a youthful and beautiful countenance, from both an outward perspective for physical beauty as well as an inner perspective for a beautiful soul. You're going to capture this energy in a sunrise, so be prepared for an early start. You will want a semiprivate outdoor area for this, either your own backyard, the backyard of an open-minded friend or family member, a semi-secluded corner of a city park at daybreak (if this feels safe and feasible to you), a favorite wilderness location if you're a hiker, or the patio or porch of your home if it faces east.

continued →

Shine Brightly as the Sunlit Power Spell *continued*

TOOLS YOU WILL NEED:

- ✳ Flowers: marigolds, sunflowers, and saffron and yellow daisies, carnations, or roses
- ✳ Incense: cedarwood, copal, or cinnamon
- ✳ Candle: 1 yellow pillar
- ✳ Essential oil: cedarwood, copal, or cinnamon
- ✳ Matches or lighter
- ✳ Small bowl of water
- ✳ Hand towel

1. This ritual is best done while sitting on the ground. Just before sunrise, arrange the flowers, herbs, and incense you have chosen in a pleasing manner for your altar.

2. Anoint the yellow pillar candle with essential oil and place it as the centerpiece of your altar area. Light the candle and incense.

3. Fill a small ceramic bowl with water, sprinkling in the flowers of your choosing into it. Have a hand towel nearby.

4. As the sun begins to rise above the horizon, hold your hands over the bowl of water, saying:

   "As the sun renews this day, so shall it renew youth and beauty to me.

   As the sun renews this day, so shall it bless my countenance with radiance."

5. Allow the rays of the sun to fall onto the bowl of water, charging it with its energy.

6. Bend over the bowl of water, and cupping your hands together, splash this energized now-magically charged water on your face several times. Use the small hand towel to pat your face dry.

7. Stand and face the sun, saying:

   "I've been kissed by the sun, it is done. So mote it be."

JUPITER'S EXPANSION SPELL

The energy of Jupiter is pregnant with possibilities for expansion. The energy of this celestial body lends itself to growth, success, over-the-top victory, and prosperity.

TOOLS YOU WILL NEED:

- ⚝ Herbs: anise, cinquefoil, hyssop, meadowsweet, or sage
- ⚝ Incense: frankincense or dragon's blood
- ⚝ Essential oil: frankincense, dragon's blood, or sage
- ⚝ Candles: 4 purple votives

- ⚝ Matches or lighter
- ⚝ 4 coins: penny, nickel, dime, and quarter
- ⚝ A small coin purse
- ⚝ A small cloth bag of gauze, cotton, or flannel

1. Set up your altar with the flowers and herbs and incense in a pleasant arrangement.

2. Anoint each of the purple candles with the essential oil of your choice, and then set them on the altar. Light the candles and incense when you're ready to begin.

3. Start by anointing yourself with the essential oil, just a touch to the inside of each wrist.

4. Touch each one of the coins with essential oil and place them in the small coin purse or clutch bag.

5. Add the herbs you chose to the small cloth mojo bag and anoint it with a touch of essential oil.

6. Add this mojo bag to the coin purse or the clutch bag.

7. Lay this purse or bag on the altar, holding your hands over it, say:

   "As the energy of Jupiter builds, we reap what we sow.

   As the night is black as the wings of the crow, as the heavens awaken with a celestial glow, riches come to me. So mote it be."

NOTES AND REFLECTIONS

NOTES AND REFLECTIONS

CHAPTER 6

Of Signs & Sigils: Divination & Sigil Magic

Viewing the shiny surfaces of objects, such as crystal balls or mirrors, in order to psychically see or gain intuitive information is called crystallomancy. This type of divination is classic and stereotypical to what many people think of when they think of the witch.

The magical practitioner also has sigils in her divination arsenal, intentionally charged symbols for the explicit purpose of magical manifestation. Through the personal creation of sigils, the green witch is empowered, taking responsibility and control over the energy and success of her spiritual practice. We're going to explore both of these spiritual tools and learn how to harness their power for our own use.

BLESSED BE THE CRYSTAL BALL

Scrying with a crystal ball activates the spiritual world and draws energies from that realm to us. These energies are not something that normally touches our world, but scrying and the tools we're using awaken the entities of this plane, drawing their attention to us. Usually these contacts are positive contacts that grant a plethora of insight, but they can also be physically draining, and sometimes even aggressive. It's advised that you do a cleansing smudge with sage on yourself before and after contacting the spirit realm with any divination tool.

FORESEE THIS FUTURE VISION RITUAL

The most popular reason for using the crystal ball is to see the future. We all want to be able to magically step beyond the bounds of time to find out what's going to happen next, before it happens, and this ritual will get you started.

TOOLS YOU WILL NEED:

- ✷ Candle: 1 white pillar
- ✷ Matches or lighter
- ✷ Sage smudge stick

- ✷ Incense: Nag Champa, sandalwood, rose, cinnamon, or an incense of your choice
- ✷ Table and chair
- ✷ Crystal ball

TO PERFORM THE RITUAL:

1. Light the white candle, smudge yourself with the sage stick, and light your incense.

2. Sit at the table with your crystal ball in front of you. Place your hands gently on the ball and allow yourself to relax.

3. If you have a particular question, formulate and focus upon it in your mind.

4. Remove your hands from the crystal ball and gaze at it. Eventually your eyes will relax, and your vision may become unfocused.

5. Some people experience the sight of smoke or fog forming within the crystal ball; allow this to happen without mentally interrupting it. Often, after the ball fills like this, images will start to form.

6. Note that some people connect with this energy more in their mind's eye than with physical visions. If this is what happens to you, allow the process to continue naturally.

7. If you are unfamiliar with scrying and divining this way, the images or symbols you see at first, either physically or psychically, may not make sense to you. If you work with this energy often enough, you will figure out your personal symbology and the messages you receive will become quite clear. Pay attention to the images you're shown and to the questions that were on your mind at that moment.

8. When you feel that your session has come to a conclusion, place your hands on the crystal ball.

9. Allow your mind and thoughts to quiet, empty, and relax. When you feel this has been accomplished, remove your hands from the crystal ball.

10. Smudge yourself.

LEARN FROM THY PAST RITUAL

Almost everyone experiences *déjà vu*, the feeling of having lived before, a feeling of familiarity with a historical time, or a familiarity with a location we've never visited. For those of us who would like to dig deeper and find out what this connection from the past means, and what we can learn from it, we're going to delve into the depths of our crystal ball.

TOOLS YOU WILL NEED:

✶ Candle: 1 white pillar

✶ Matches or lighter

✶ Sage smudge stick

✶ Table and chair

✶ Crystal ball

✶ Pen and notebook (optional)

continued →

Learn from Thy Past Ritual *continued*

TO PERFORM THE RITUAL:

1. Light the white candle, smudge yourself with the sage stick, and light your incense.

2. Sit at the table with your crystal ball in front of you. Place your hands gently on the ball and relax.

3. When you've reached a relaxed state, remove your hands from the crystal ball. While gazing upon it, allow your mind to gently drift to those times in history, places, and *déjà vu* memories that persist for you.

4. As you are connecting with these images, either as a visual inside the crystal ball or as psychic images, allow them to expand and follow through as you would while watching a movie.

5. This part is optional: Some of us can stay immersed within this relaxed alpha state and still maintain enough connection with our conscious mind so that we can pick up a pen and write down the information we're receiving without breaking our concentration. If you can do this, have a pen and notebook handy.

6. When you feel that your session is coming to a close, place your hands on the crystal ball and allow your mind to become still and centered. Once you've reached this point, remove your hands from the crystal ball.

7. Smudge yourself.

CONNECTING WITH A DECEASED LOVED ONE

Crystal balls are a gateway to the Spirit world, which makes them the perfect divination tool for connecting with a loved one who has passed. Even if you've never experienced mediumship abilities, the odds are that you will be able to forge this spirit connection with the aid of this divination tool.

TOOLS YOU WILL NEED:

- Candle: 1 white pillar
- Matches or lighter
- Sage smudge stick
- Incense: Nag Champa, sage, sandalwood, or a scent of your own choosing

- Table and chair
- Crystal ball
- A photo of your deceased loved one or an item that belonged to them (optional)

TO PERFORM THE RITUAL:

1. Light the white candle, smudge yourself with the sage stick, and light your incense.

2. Sit at the table with your crystal ball in front of you. Place your loved one's photo or item on the table, if you choose. Place your hands on the ball until you reach a state of relaxation.

3. Once you've reached this state, remove your hands from the crystal ball. Gaze at the ball and formulate an image of your loved one in your mind. Allow whatever sequence of images, or even audio experiences, that arise to move along in an uninterrupted state. Pay attention to what you're shown and to what you hear, both physically and psychically. Pay attention to any physical stimulation or feelings, like hot or cold, or warming or tingly sensations.

4. When you feel that your session has come to a conclusion, place your hands on the crystal ball, bid your loved one farewell, and allow your mind to become focused and return to a fully conscious state.

5. Smudge yourself.

CRAFT A SCRYING MIRROR

The tradition of the scrying mirror, or the "magic mirror," is an old one. Reputedly, it was this divination tool that Nostradamus used for his now infamous predictions. The scrying mirror is a witch's favorite for delving into the past, present, and future in search of hidden information. Creating your own scrying mirror is simple and will also ensure that your mirror will be filled with your own energy to tap into for psychic insights.

TOOLS YOU WILL NEED:

⋆ A picture frame or a hand mirror with a dark frame, no larger than 12 inches in diameter

⋆ Black paint or spray paint with a high-gloss enamel (a glossy sheen is essential)

⋆ A soft cleaning cloth

⋆ A cloth bag large enough to hold your scrying mirror

TO CRAFT THE MIRROR:

1. Clean the glass surface of the picture frame or mirror.

2. Remove the glass from the picture frame to spray-paint it. Tape the frame on the mirror when you spray-paint it to protect it.

3. Let dry.

4. You can leave your mirror to set in the rays of the moon on a full-moon night to consecrate it.

5. Keep your mirror's surface clean using a soft cloth and keep it safe in a cloth bag when not in use.

UNFOG MY OUTLOOK CLARITY RITUAL

How ironic is it that to see something clearly you will be looking into the blackness of a scrying mirror? This divination tool works very similarly to the crystal ball, in that some people see visions with their eyes on the surface of the mirror, and others experience this psychically through clairvoyance, clairaudience, or clairsentience. May you lose yourself in the depth of this ritual and come away with a fresh outlook and new perspective.

TOOLS YOU WILL NEED:

* Candle: 1 white pillar
* Matches or lighter
* Sage smudge stick
* Incense: sage, sandalwood, cinnamon, or a scent of your choice
* Table and chair
* Scrying mirror (page 148)

TO PERFORM THE RITUAL:

1. Light the white candle, smudge yourself with the sage stick, and light your incense.

2. Darken the room.

3. Sit at the table with your scrying mirror in front of you. Place the candle very close to the mirror, so that the flame reflects off its surface.

4. Lay both hands on the table, palms up, and gaze into the surface of the mirror until your mind begins to relax and be still, and your vision becomes slightly unfocused.

5. As you feel yourself drifting into this state, bring forward in your thoughts the issues that need clarity.

6. When the visions begin to appear on the surface of the mirror or within your mind's eye, allow them to flow freely with no interruption or interference.

7. When you feel that this session is coming to a close, the energy and visions receding, allow it to do so naturally, placing your hands on the table, palms down.

8. Smudge yourself.

SEE PAST THE PAIN CLEANSING RITUAL

In order to see past the pain in your life, you're going to have to examine exactly what is causing it. Before you begin this scrying ritual, sit down with paper and pen and list exactly what it is that you need to dismiss from your life to allow healing.

TOOLS YOU WILL NEED:

- ✶ Candle: 1 white pillar
- ✶ Matches or lighter
- ✶ Sage smudge stick
- ✶ Table and chair
- ✶ Scrying mirror (page 148)
- ✶ Pen and paper
- ✶ Fireproof plate

TO PERFORM THE RITUAL:

1. Light the white candle and smudge yourself with the sage stick.

2. Darken the room.

3. Sit at the table with your scrying mirror in front of you. Place the lit candle close to the mirror so that the light reflects on the surface.

4. Lay the sheet of paper on the table, folded so that the writing is inward, close to the mirror.

5. Lay both hands on the table, palms up, and ready yourself to relax, allowing your gaze to focus on the surface of the mirror.

6. Once you've achieved a relaxed state, open yourself up to the possibilities of the mirror and the inner dialogue you've been having with yourself over specific issues.

7. Allow the images of the mirror, or your psychic mind, to move through undisturbed.

8. When it feels that this state is coming to a conclusion but has not quite ended, and you're able to concentrate, pick up the paper and hold it to the candle flame.

9. Allow the paper to catch fire and drop it onto the fireproof plate, where it can continue to burn to ash.

10. Smudge yourself.

11. Dispose of the ash by tossing it into the wind.

BLACK MIRROR REVERSAL SPELL

TOOLS YOU WILL NEED:

* Candle: 1 white pillar
* Matches or lighter
* Sage smudging stick
* Sea salt

* Stones: 3, 6, or 9 black obsidian
* Incense: dragon's blood, patchouli, rosemary, or a scent of your choice
* Table and chair
* Scrying mirror (page 148)

1. Light the white candle.

2. Smudge yourself with the sage stick.

3. Darken the room.

4. Sprinkle sea salt around the base of the white candle, and arrange the stones of black obsidian around the base of the candle. Light the incense.

5. Sit at your table with the scrying mirror in front of you.

6. Evoke the spirits of the ethereal realm, saying:

   "By cast and stone and bone, by all that eat the flesh of death, by all that ravage the putrid breath; by cast and stone and bone, come through this mirror, come to atone."

7. Lay your hands on the table, palms up, and gaze upon the mirror until you reach a relaxed state and your vision is beginning to be somewhat blurry and unfocused.

8. Stay alert enough to ask questions and receive answers. Stay alert enough to also direct the spirits to reverse the energy that was manifested in the casting of a spell.

9. When you feel you've accomplished your goal and the energy of the mirror is fading, dismiss the spirits, saying:

   "By cast and stone and bone, I dismiss you now, be gone, leave me alone."

10. Smudge yourself.

SEE THE SIGIL ANEW

A sigil is an intention that is created and condensed into a single glyph. It's created by placing the letters of the alphabet in a circle or wheel in a pattern within it and using a pen or pencil to connect the letters that spell out your intention.

The design this creates is your personal sigil, which can be used for spell crafting by carving it into candles, using it to empower objects, or placing it on your altar for magical manifestation or meditation. Creating a sigil allows you to use your own creative energy, be decisive, be motivated, and direct in your spiritual practice.

The sigil for the following rituals was created with the word *manifestation* from a sigil wheel much like the one shown on page 142 in the opening illustration.

DIVINING A SIGIL FOR DEVOTION

Loyalty and devotion may be the most profound and necessary attributes to make a relationship successful and fulfilling, and this includes romantic, friendship, or familial relationships.

TOOLS YOU WILL NEED:

☆ Candle: 1 white pillar

☆ Essential oil: rose, gardenia, or jasmine

☆ Matches or lighter

☆ Table

☆ Paper with image of sigil drawn on it, no larger than 3-by-5 inches

☆ Stone: 6 small rose quartz stones

☆ A small white bag, gauze or cotton

1. Anoint your white pillar candle with essential oil, place it on the table, and light it.

2. Write the name of the individual you're targeting for this ritual on top of the sigil, and place this paper beneath the candle.

3. Place the rose quartz stones around the base of the candle.

4. Burn this candle for an hour each day for six days.

5. On the sixth day, extinguish the flame, remove the sigil paper from beneath the candle, place it in a small white bag, and keep it tucked in a safe place, such as a bureau drawer or your closet.

DIVINING A SIGIL FOR COURAGE

Telling someone they need to suck it up and find the courage to confront something, or to do something that is unnerving and challenging, is so much easier said than done. Sometimes we all need an extra boost of magical courage to face life's tribulations. This sigil will help provide that magical boost.

TOOLS YOU WILL NEED:

⚹ Paper with this sigil drawn on it, the size of a sticky note, approximately 3-by-3½ inches

⚹ Pen or pencil

⚹ Essential oil: dragon's blood, cloves, or cedar

1. The night before you're set to do, say, face, start, or finish something that is very daunting for you, take a small piece of paper with this sigil drawn on it, write the word *courage* on top of the sigil, and anoint it with essential oil.

2. Sleep with this piece of paper in your pillowcase.

3. The next day, place the paper in your pocket, carrying it on you.

DIVINING A SIGIL FOR A WITCH'S FATED PURPOSE

At some point, all of us on this spiritual path wonder what our purpose is. What are your special gifts? What seems to be your natural talent? How do you know where your power resides, and how you can manifest that energy into the real world? Sometimes those great big questions take a little ritual in order to uncover the answers.

TOOLS YOU WILL NEED:

⚹ Candle: 1 white pillar

⚹ Essential oil: patchouli, sage, or eucalyptus

⚹ Table

⚹ Matches or lighter

⚹ Paper with image of sigil drawn on it, no larger than 3-by-5 inches

⚹ Stones: 3 white selenite stones or 3 clear quartz crystal stones

⚹ Small white gauze or cotton bag

continued →

Divining a Sigil for a Witch's Fated Purpose *continued*

1. Anoint your white candle with essential oil, set it on the table, and light it.

2. Across the top of the sigil paper, write: *"Reveal my gift to me, in dreams of three."*

3. Place this paper beneath the candle.

4. Place the stones around the base of the candle.

5. For three nights, burn this candle an hour before you go to bed.

6. On the morning of the fourth day, gather the stones and place them in a small white bag. Keep this bag in your pillowcase.

7. Pay attention to your dreams; this is where your answers will be revealed.

DIVINING A SIGIL FOR EMPLOYMENT

Competition in the workforce is fierce. Along with that fact comes the daunting tasks of filling out applications and successfully navigating the crucial interview process. Using this manifestation sigil, we'll give ourselves a leg up on this modern-day conundrum.

TOOLS YOU WILL NEED:

- ✴ **Paper with your sigil drawn on it, no larger than 3-by-3 inches**
- ✴ **A fireproof plate**
- ✴ **Candles: 1 white votive, 1 black votive, and 1 yellow votive**
- ✴ **Herbs: eyebright, mint, or anise**
- ✴ **Stones: 3 small tiger's eye**
- ✴ **Essential oils: patchouli, sage, or sandalwood**
- ✴ **Incense: cinnamon or patchouli**
- ✴ **Matches or lighter**
- ✴ **Small white gauze bag**

1. Place the sigil on a fireproof plate.

2. Inscribe this sigil on all three candles and place them on the plate on top of the paper with the yellow candle in the middle.

3. Sprinkle the herbs around the base of the candles.

4. Anoint the stones and place them around the base of the candles.

5. Light the candles and incense.

6. Allow them to burn down.

7. Gather the remnants of this spell—the candle wax, herbs, and stones—and place them in the gauze bag.

8. Keep this bag near your computer when filling out applications, and carry this bag on you, tucked into a pocket or bag, when you go for an interview.

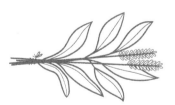

SIGNS AND SIGILS PRACTICE

SIGNS AND SIGILS PRACTICE

CHAPTER 7

Wield Wisely the Wood: Handcrafts & Charms with Natural Materials

Just as the green witch embraces the energy of flowers and herbs, they also recognize the magic imbued in various types of wood. Whether they're creating a magic wand, a box, or a broom, or using wood in some other magical endeavor, the green witch is familiar with the various types of energies connected to specific trees, and they know how to harness this energy for their own use. Here, we'll explore some of these types and energies to help center and ground your own practice within the world of wood.

WHICH WOOD FOR THE WITCH?

Use this helpful guide to steer you toward the wood that's perfect for your ritual, spell, or magical work.

Applewood: Applewood is connected to the feminine divine. It enhances fertility, peace, and joy and it makes powerful magic when working with fairies and love. Applewood also promotes visions.

Birch: Birch is used in cleansing and exorcism rituals. Its energy lends itself to rebirth and renewal and is often used for healing the body and calming the mind. Birch energy also blesses new beginnings, new starts, and new endeavors.

Black walnut: Black walnut is an excellent wood to use for astral travel, teleportation, as well as weather magic, where its power lies in the wind and the ability to provide protection from lightning.

Cedar: Cedarwood cleanses negative atmospheres and is used for the creation of sacred space. Its energy lends itself to protection and longevity. This wood is used in rituals and invocations to evoke spirits.

Elm: Elm wood is used for magic pertaining to death and rebirth, stability, grounding, and fairy magic. It is used during the invocation of the feminine divine, and it lends itself to endurance and rituals for women in the crone stage of life.

Hawthorn: Hawthorn provides psychic protection. This wood lends itself to spells that boost self-confidence and build a personality full of charm. Hawthorn enhances beguiling moods and encourages patience and creativity.

Lilac: Lilac wood is full of energy for love, romance, and passion. It is used in spells to enhance a sexual relationship, as well as spells for protection during travel, and illusion.

Maple: Maple's energy lends itself to intellect, communication, and mental concentration. It enhances spells for creativity, binding, as well as intellectual pursuits, art, and abundance.

Oak: Oak is considered the most powerful wood magically. The energy of oak is used for spells that involve time and counter spells to undo magic, either your own or someone else's. It's also used to center the mind, silence distractions, and heal and promote longevity, prosperity, and strength.

Palm: Palm is noted for its durability and the ability to withstand time. This wood is self-renewing and it aids in rejuvenation and longevity.

Pine: Pine is one of the few trees that are androgynous. This wood is a symbol for life and carries the energy of immortality, peace, and serenity. Pine can alleviate the emotion of guilt.

Rowan: Rowan protects against negative enchantments. This wood also lends its energy for healing, divination and psychic enhancement.

White ash: White ash is filled with energy for protection, spirituality, healing, justice, and wisdom. This wood is used in spells to mend emotional rifts and instigate communication.

Willow: Willow aligns itself with healing, emotions, renewed vitality, divination, and heightened intuition. This wood strengthens the third eye and enhances any form of divination.

Yew: Yew is also known as the world tree. Its energy is connected to death and rebirth. This wood enhances psychic abilities and it promotes visions.

What are some other wood types you use in your magic?

_____

_____

_____

_____

_____

CRAFTY BE THE WITCH

Spell casting and magical manifestation are all about moving energy. The work that goes into gathering ingredients and supplies, the process of handcrafting magical objects, and the end result that's put to magical use are all highlights of the green witch and their spiritual path. The energy that they produce in these endeavors leads to a successful spell or ritual. Within this section, we're going to try our hand at being a crafty witch and produce magical items for luck and blessings.

LIVE LONG THE LUCK HERB SACHET

This is a sachet to bring you luck, good health, and many blessings. It will be small enough to carry in a purse or pocket, or keep it in a bureau or desk drawer, the glove compartment of your vehicle, or in your pillowcase.

TOOLS YOU WILL NEED:

* Material of your choice, such as flannel, cotton, or gauze, no larger than 3-by-5 inches
* Needle and thread
* Herbs: lavender, rosemary, and whole allspice
* Stones: small tiger's eye
* A small religious medallion of your choice, such as a pentacle, a cross, a star of David, or another symbol that you connect with
* Essential oil: rosemary, eucalyptus, or sandalwood

1. Fold the piece of cloth in half. Using a needle and thread, sew two sides of the cloth shut to form a bag with the top remaining open.

2. Place into the bag the herbs, stone, and religious medallion.

3. Add 3 to 8 drops of essential oil to the contents.

4. Sew up the top of the bag, sealing it shut.

LAVENDER OIL BLESSED CELTIC CROSS

Some people believe that the Celtic cross was originally a symbol for the Roman sun god Invictus, while others believe the halo on the cross represents Christ, and some believe that the Celtic cross is a long-lost symbol from the ancient Pagan days. Whatever this symbol represents to you, it's old, full of energy, and very powerful.

The following ritual is a spiritual blessing and empowerment for a Celtic cross pendant. You can also use this spell to bless a pentacle or pentagram pendant you wear. If you choose to wear a symbol like these, you can use this ritual to focus its energy on you, your life, and your spiritual path. You'll create a sacred box to keep your pendant in when you're not wearing it.

TOOLS YOU WILL NEED:

- ⚹ Wooden box from a craft or hobby shop
- ⚹ Paint, any color of your choice
- ⚹ Paintbrushes
- ⚹ Small cloth, 2-by-2 inches
- ⚹ Essential oil: lavender
- ⚹ A Celtic cross pendant

1. Decorate the wooden box by painting it a color, or colors, of your choosing.

2. Place several drops of lavender essential oil on a small cloth and place this cloth in the box.

3. You can reinfuse this cloth with the lavender oil on a regular basis to keep the energy and the scent alive, perhaps once a month.

4. The first time you wear your pendant, anoint it with lavender oil, saying:

   *"With this oil, I anoint thee; bring blessings
   and protection to me."*

MINI-BROOM FOR HOUSEHOLD BLESSINGS

The green witch's magical broom, also known as a *besom,* is often used to ritualistically create sacred space, clear negative energies from a house, and provide blessings and protection. There are versions of the magic broom that can be used in ways that bring very specific energies of protection and blessings to your home. It comes in the form of a very small broom, which can

continued →

Mini-Broom for Household Blessings *continued*

be purchased at your local craft or hobby shop and decorated, blessed, and hung over your front door.

TOOLS YOU WILL NEED:

- A small broom
- Colored ribbons, in widths and colors of your choice:
- Green, for health and prosperity
- Red or pink, for love and passion
- Black, for protection in the physical realm
- White, for protection in the spiritual realm
- Blue, to connect with spirits and entities of the ethereal world
- Yellow, to advance creativity and communication
- Essential oil: sage, rosemary, peppermint, or cedar
- Small bowl of coarse sea salt
- Incense: sandalwood, dragon's blood, or eucalyptus
- Candle: 1 white votive
- Small bowl of water

1. Tie the ribbon to your chosen broom in whatever fashion you choose, either with streamers allowed to hang from the broom or crisscrossed down the handle.

2. Anoint your broom with essential oil.

3. When you've finished decorating your broom, it will be time to consecrate it: Sprinkle a pinch of coarse sea salt on the bristles of the broom, saying:

   "By the energy of earth, bless and protect my physical world from anything or anyone who may damage it."

4. Pass incense over the bristles of your broom, saying:

   "By the energy of air, bless and protect my mental world from anything or anyone who may damage it."

5. Hold a lit white candle over your broom, saying:

   "By the power of fire, bless and protect my passion and motivation from anyone or anything that may damage it."

6. Dip your fingers in the bowl of water and sprinkle it onto the bristles of your broom, saying:

"By the energy of water, protect my emotions and my heart from anyone or anything that may damage it. By the elements, this broom is now consecrated and blessed, charged to protect me and my household."

MINI ALTAR KIT

The green witch often leads a busy life, so being able to keep connected to her spiritual practice is a key issue. This kit will come in handy when you're away from home and need to cast a quick spell, acknowledge a powerful moon phase, or simply to connect with the divine.

Add something to this mini altar kit that connects with each of the four elements. For example: stones for earth, a small feather for air, whole cloves to represent fire, and a small seashell to represent water.

TOOLS YOU WILL NEED:

- ⚹ A small wooden box or cardboard box suitable for jewelry
- ⚹ Stones: a small stone, or stones, of your choice: green stones for health, healing, and prosperity; red stones for passion and action; yellow stones for communication and creativity; blue stones for emotion, dream enhancement, and psychic awareness; and black stones for protection.
- ⚹ A feather
- ⚹ Herbs: whole cloves
- ⚹ A small seashell
- ⚹ Candle: 1 tealight candle
- ⚹ Matches or small lighter
- ⚹ An incense cone, the scent of your choice: rose for love and relationships, patchouli for physical issues, frankincense for financial help, sage or rosemary for cleansing, or Nag Champa as an all-around incense to cover divine connections and secret desires
- ⚹ A quarter
- ⚹ A religious medallion or talisman of your choice (optional)

1. In a small wooden box, place the stones, a feather, herbs, a seashell a tealight candle, and a small book of matches or small lighter.

2. Add an incense cone and a quarter to set it on when you light it.

3. Add the small medallion or pendant that represents your spiritual path.

Conclusion

Congratulations on taking your first steps toward green witchcraft with this grimoire. You've made impressive strides as you've worked your way through these pages. It takes courage and conviction to step out on a solitary spiritual journey and embrace new ideas and practices. As you continue this journey, doors to magical knowledge and enlightenment will continue to open for you.

For most of us who discover witchcraft, it feels like coming home. *"There's a little witch in every woman,"* to quote Aunt Jett from the movie *Practical Magic.* Actually, there's a little witch in **all** of us, and most people drawn to this path are already aware of these energies; they just don't understand what they're all about until something shines a light upon them . . . like a book.

Know that this spiritual path involves a lifetime of exploration and practice. It's an ongoing process of learning, and you will be referring to this grimoire, and your own notes, again and again as you embrace the magic. In joy and wonder, continue your growth on the path of the green witch. Share with others what you've learned, and celebrate your spiritual milestones. Blessed be!

Resources

Cunningham, Scott. *The Complete Book of Incense Oils & Brews.* St. Paul, MN: Llewellyn Publications, 2002.

Cunningham, Scott. *Cunningham's Encyclopedia of Crystal, Gem & Metal Magic.* St. Paul, MN: Llewellyn Publications, 2004.

Cunningham, Scott. *Cunningham's Encyclopedia of Magical Herbs.* St. Paul, MN: Llewellyn Publications, 2002.

Cunningham, Scott. *Cunningham's Encyclopedia of Wicca in the Kitchen.* St. Paul, MN: Llewellyn Publications, 2002.

Scott Cunningham's books are classic. You'll be able to find the most basic information on herbs, stones, and potions in his books. This beloved pagan author left the world far too soon, but his legacy will continue as his books line the shelves of pagan homes around the world. He takes the mundane and transforms it into the magical. Through his kitchen book, our love of food is elevated to a spiritual level filled with infinite possibilities and powerful manifestation.

Hall, Judy. *The Encyclopedia of Crystals.* Beverly, MA: Fair Winds Press, 2006.

This is your go-to book for geographical, medicinal, and magical information for almost any crystal or stone that you can think of. This book is color-coded and contains two indexes. At the front of the book is an index of stones by name; at the back of the book is an index of their uses.

Martine Woolfolk, Joanna. *The Only Astrology Book You'll Ever Need.* Lanham, MD: Madison Books, 2001.

This is an apt title. Everything I've ever needed to know about astrology I've found in this book, such as extraordinary tables to help you calculate your own birth chart, including your sun, moon, and rising signs.

Yronwode, Catherine. *Hoodoo Herb and Root Magic.* Forestville, CA: The Lucky Mojo Curio Co., 2002.

Catherine is a classic hoodoo lady who started her practice in the 1970s. This book contains a plethora of information on folklore and spells.

Glossary

Amulet: A magically empowered object that deflects specific, usually negative, energy.

Asperging: Sprinkling water or smoke around a space for blessing or cleansing, while using herbs, tools, or fingers.

Athame: A ritual knife used only to direct energy, particularly when casting a circle to create sacred space.

Banish: The magical act of driving away evil or negativity. It is also sending away someone or something that is not healthy or desirable for you.

Bolline: A working knife used to cut string, cord, and herbs, as well as to carve sigils and symbols.

Book of Shadows: A book containing your spells, lists of herbs and stones, and many personal references to your craft, life, and path. This is a book that is most often kept secret and not shared with anyone.

Conjuring: Creating an entity or manifestation through the use of spells and magic.

Consecration: A ritual of sanctification or purification. Also, a ritual of dedication, usually for an object.

Coven: A group of at least three, and no more than 13, witches led by a high priest or priestess.

Deosil: A clockwise movement.

Divination: The art of foretelling the future, as well as tapping into intuition and psychic awareness through the means of tools such as tarot cards, runes, and crystal balls.

Esbat: A pagan ritual to celebrate a full moon.

Familiar: An animal with a special spiritual connection to a witch, who often lends their energies to her spell crafting. The cat has long been the most popular familiar depicted in modern media.

Herb: A plant used in magic for its energy, whether flowers, grasses, vegetables, fruits, or spices.

Meditation: Contemplation and reflection during a still and focused moment. It is also a personal quiet time set aside for deep thought open to spiritual enlightenment.

Mojo bag: A small bag made of cloth or leather that will hold crystals, herbs, and other magical items.

Pagan: A term to describe individuals from a variety of spiritual paths that are nature-based, often incorporating magic spells, polytheistic deities (gods and goddesses) from a plethora of cultures, as well as rites and rituals outside the more common Judeo-Christian culture.

Pentagram/pentacle: A five-pointed star representing the four elements (earth, air, fire, and water), and Spirit. A pentagram is enclosed in a circle, while a pentacle is not.

Sabbat: A pagan holiday; the eight pagan holidays are Samhain, Yule, Imbolc, Ostara, Beltane, Summer Solstice, Lammas, and Mabon.

Spell: A magical ritual to move energy and create manifestation, usually accompanied by the use of objects such as herbs, candles, oils, etc., and sometimes incorporating the use of spoken words.

Summerland: A peaceful place the spirit of someone who's passed can reside until ready for a reincarnation. It is also often viewed by some traditions as the pagan version of heaven.

Talisman: An object empowered to attract particular energies.

Ward: To place magical boundaries of protection around a property or sacred space.

Widdershins: A counterclockwise movement.

Witch: An individual who practices ancient folk magic that predates Christianity, which includes herbalism, divination, spells, as well as some holistic healing methods. A witch can be either a man or a woman.

Index

Acknowledgments

I want to thank my editor, Jesse, and the other amazing people who put work and effort into the creation of this book. Your enthusiasm, support, and hard work are what made this project possible. This was a magical journey of love for the pagan community and the green witches of the world.

About the Author

AMYTHYST RAINE is a published author under Labyrinth House, Moon Books, Dodona Books, and Amazon. She's a professional tarot reader and a practicing witch living in the Sonoran Desert in Arizona.

CPSIA information can be obtained
at www.ICGtesting.com
Printed in the USA
JSHW042151020720
6450JS00003B/65